BlueGhost Reveille

D1637541

J O H N   W .   H A R R I S

PAGE PUBLISHING, INC.
New York, NY

First originally published by Page Publishing, Inc. 2018

ISBN 978-1-64350-398-1 (Paperback)
ISBN 978-1-64350-399-8 (Digital)

Printed in the United States of America

Contents

Foreword

The idea for writing these thoughts regarding my Vietnam experience came from my daughter, Jennifer. She gave a small book to me that consisted mostly of thirty-eight questions with space to write in answers. Questions like "What was your first car and how much did it cost?" and "What was your first job and how much were you paid?"

This prompted me to sit down and write for the first time in a long time. The reaction to this within my family was very gratifying, but it made me a little sad that my parents or grandparents never did this for my sisters and me.

My grandson, Frankie, has asked questions about the experience of war. My attendance at F Troop Eighth Cavalry BlueGhost reunions has spurred many memories regarding the war. At these reunions, it has been good for me to talk with people who shared these events. All these things motivated me to get these remembrances on paper before my mind starts to slide or the great time keeper in the sky says game over. After all, I am seventy as I write this.

Another thing I want to emphasize is that these are my thoughts and memories. One thing that has become very clear from my meetings and conversations with BlueGhost veterans is that people recall events differently. There is no intentional fiction in these pieces. They are sincerely from my heart and mind as factually as I remember them.

The bulk of this writing is from my time in country. There are a few pieces from post-war times including reunion notes, stories about Roger Caruthers, and so on. *Why Did You Go and Leave Me?* was written about twenty-five years after I had been home. As I was riding down the road, something made me pull over and write it, and

I did it in about five minutes. It was kept in a folder until the writing of these pieces in the last three months.

My daughter Stephanie has done the typing for this effort, and she has assisted in editing. Both my daughters, Stephanie and Jennifer, have been encouraging through everything, and I am very proud to be their dad.

My wife, Eve, has gotten to know many of the BlueGhost men, their spouses, and children. She loves them and they have taken her to heart. Her encouragement and patience have pushed this project down the track, and as always, I'm lucky to have her on my side.

My Army Start

My two-year career in the Army started as a draftee. One of those letters came in the mail in May 1968, and it said, "Greetings, you will report to the Induction Center on Ponce De Leon Avenue in Atlanta, Georgia."

Basic training was a nighttime bus ride away from Atlanta to Fort Benning in Columbus, Georgia. Nobody was happy to be there as we arrived in the predawn hours. The first thing we did was get off the bus, form up a line, and walk across a parking lot picking up cigarette butts. You could just tell this was going to be great fun.

We next got assigned to drill sergeants who "lovingly" took us under their wings. We got called more names than I knew existed. They cut our hair down to the skull, and then we went to get our Army uniforms. When we finished getting all our issue clothes and were going to leave the building, there was a sign telling us that we were now "part of the best dressed Army in the world." Somehow "best dressed" was not a feeling I shared at the time.

The sergeants worked us hard. There was a lot of PT, physical training, that truly did get us into pretty good physical shape. They taught us to shoot and clean rifles and work with the Army gear. The main thing they were doing was tearing us down as individuals and putting us back together as a unit. Let's face it, to function as an Army, it has to be that way.

Upon completing basic, I was sent to Fort Ord, California, for AIT, Advanced Individual Training. My specialty, along with most everybody else, was Infantry. My ticket to Vietnam was already pretty well punched.

We did arrive at Fort Ord dressed for the occasion, thanks to a drill sergeant at Fort Benning who had spent time at Fort Ord and knew the climate there was very different. Everyone who was assigned to Fort Polk, Louisiana; Fort Jackson, South Carolina; or elsewhere was told to dress in short-sleeved khaki uniforms. It was late summer or early fall and still hot. He told us to wear dress greens.

As I said earlier, the climate on the California coast around Fort Ord is unique. We arrived in the middle of the night, and it was cold. The days could be warm to hot and the nights always cool. The thing that was most noticeable was that during the day, when we were doing PT (physical training), classes, or shooting ranges, you could see fog rolling off the Pacific, and when it got to us, the temperature would drop precipitously. As the sun burned off the fog, the temperature would jump back up. It changed enough so that the instructors would stop what they were doing and have us take off our field jacket, or put them back on as the fog and the temperature dictated.

Mark Twain spent some time in San Francisco, which is just north of Fort Ord, and he famously said that the coldest winter he ever spent was a summer in San Francisco.

Things remembered about being in Fort Ord was that marching or running were tough, because it was done on the beaches as much as possible. The rest of the area was very sandy, so it seemed like every time you took a step forward, you slid half a step back. It was tough on the body and legs, but we got into good shape. Another thing about Ord was that the food was awful. The food at Fort Benning seemed like a banquet next to Ord.

On the positive side, I met some good people. Two of them were from southern California down around Los Angeles. Larry Larson was one fellow's name, and the other I can't remember his name. They both had been teachers and were drafted. The one whose name I can't recall taught California history. They were in my platoon and we did a lot of training together, so it was natural that we did some weekend pass stuff together too. We went to a museum in

Monterey that was of interest because the history teacher was taking pictures and gathering historical information to use when he returned to teaching. Monterey had been the capital of California when the Spanish ruled the area.

The director of the museum was so impressed by my friends that he lent us his car to tour around Monterey, Carmel, Pebble Beach, and Salinas. Having cars on post during AIT was not allowed. We went all over the place during weekend passes, and I learned a lot about the area and its history. These were truly nice guys and I lost track of them. I don't know if they survived Vietnam. I sure hope they did.

At Fort Ord, I met again with Allen Caldwell and William Blanton, two Georgia boys. Allen was from Columbus and William from Griffin. We were all chosen to go to Non-Commissioned Officer (NCO) School back at Fort Benning. These are two of the finest people I have had the privilege to know. William made it through Vietnam, but sadly, Allen was killed in Vietnam in November 1969. More about that later.

Another event at Fort Ord that I hope is a once-in-a-lifetime experience was an outbreak of spinal meningitis. They say this can happen when a lot of people are in close proximity to each other. The symptoms can seem sort of like cold or flu, but they advance quickly and are very contagious. Our sleeping arrangements were bunk beds in open barracks. They had us put up sheets between each set of bunk beds, and they sent anyone with even the slightest symptoms to the hospital. One person in the battalion died during this episode. It was a strange feeling to be "afraid" of something airborne and of everyone around you.

One more experience at Ord that was new to me was the first time I had gotten over served. In other words, drunk. About halfway through AIT, we got the orders list that showed that practically all of us were going to Vietnam as infantrymen. That is not the happiest news you can get, but we all felt certain that was the way it was going to be. Well, that can be a real downer, so the next weekend pass, several of us decided to go to Carmel and buy some wine, cheese, and French bread. We took these items to a beach that faced across a small bay at Pebble Beach Golf Course. We proceeded to sit on the beach and drink our wine, eat cheese and bread until walking was optional. This was on a Saturday, and it took all Sunday to recover. Getting orders to go to a hot war as an infantryman is a hard feeling to define. Don't know if I'll ever find the words.

They tried to talk me into going to Officer Candidate School (OCS), but I would have had to extend my Army "career" from two years to three, and I was not inclined to do that. Instead, they sent me back to Benning for NCO school. This was a great learning experience and good training for the war I was definitely going to. We were trained by Rangers who had just finished tours in Vietnam.

One of the statements I remember most was "Listen up, you dumb bastards. I just did this in Vietnam four months ago, and if you don't listen and learn, you will get bagged up and sent home." This intense training lasted three months and then I was a "shake and bake" E-5 infantry sergeant. This meant I would be a squad leader in Vietnam. As a "shake and bake," we would encounter some harassment from some of the lifer types because we made rank so fast.

My reaction to this was to wish them a fast ride on the train to hell. If it had not been for the "instant NCOs," the war would have gone a lot harder for many infantrymen. The training we got from the Rangers paid off when things got dicey.

Earlier, I mentioned Allen Caldwell and I said I would talk about his death. Well, here it is. Allen was an infantry sergeant in a unit along with William Blanton in the First Infantry Division (the Big Red One). Allen had a brother named Kenny who got into the Army after Allen had been drafted. The Army had a policy that they would not allow brothers to serve in Vietnam at the same time. This was done to avoid parents having to endure the loss of two siblings at the same time (see the Sullivan brothers).

Allen was in Vietnam as an infantryman, one of the riskiest occupations possible. Kenny had gotten into helicopter maintenance, and he volunteered to go to Vietnam. The idea was that he would be in a much-safer situation, and Allen would be sent home when Kenny got to Vietnam.

It was all going as planned, and Kenny had expedited his assignment to Vietnam because Allen had already been there for three months and had been in a lot of combat. Kenny arrived in country, but the word was late getting to Allen's unit. Allen went out on a mission on the day he should have been headed home. He was killed on that mission. This mission is explained in a chapter in the book titled "Low-Level Hell."

The Army sent Kenny to accompany Allen's body back to Columbus, Georgia. It was such a shame that Allen didn't make it through. He was truly a great guy. I often wonder what his life would have been like had he not died.

He is buried at the Fort Benning Cemetery. Whenever I am in the Columbus area, I try to go by and visit with my friend. I don't know how much it helps, but it sure helps me.

SELECTIVE SERVICE SYSTEM

Approval Not Required.

ORDER TO REPORT FOR INDUCTION

The President of the United States,

LOCAL BOARD NO. 63
FULTON COUNTY
904 WEST PEACHTREE ST., N.W.
ATLANTA, GEORGIA 30309
(LOCAL BOARD STAMP)

To   JOHN WINZOR HARRIS
1890 Myrtle Drive, S. W., Apt. 114
Atlanta, Georgia 30311

MAY 9 1968
(Date of mailing)

SELECTIVE SERVICE NO.			
9	63	47	775

GREETING:

You are hereby ordered for induction into the Armed Forces of the United States, and to report

at   699 Ponce de Leon Ave., N. E., Atlanta, Georgia (Second floor)
(Place of reporting).

on MAY 2 3 1968   at   7:00 a.m.
(Date)   (Hour)

for forwarding to an Armed Forces Induction Station.

E. E. Baker
(Member or clerk of Local Board)

IMPORTANT NOTICE
(Read Each Paragraph Carefully)

IF YOU HAVE HAD PREVIOUS MILITARY SERVICE, OR ARE NOW A MEMBER OF THE NATIONAL GUARD OR A RESERVE COMPONENT OF THE ARMED FORCES, BRING EVIDENCE WITH YOU. IF YOU WEAR GLASSES, BRING THEM. IF MARRIED, BRING PROOF OF YOUR MARRIAGE. IF YOU HAVE ANY PHYSICAL OR MENTAL CONDITION WHICH, IN YOUR OPINION, MAY DISQUALIFY YOU FOR SERVICE IN THE ARMED FORCES, BRING A PHYSICIAN'S CERTIFICATE DESCRIBING THAT CONDITION, IF NOT ALREADY FURNISHED TO YOUR LOCAL BOARD.

Valid documents are required to substantiate dependency claims in order to receive basic allowance for quarters. Be sure to take the following with you when reporting to the induction station. The documents will be returned to you. (a) FOR LAWFUL WIFE OR LEGITIMATE CHILD UNDER 21 YEARS OF AGE—original, certified copy or photostat of a certified copy of marriage certificate, child's birth certificate, or a public or church record of marriage issued over the signature and seal of the custodian of the church or public records; (b) FOR LEGALLY ADOPTED CHILD—certified court order of adoption; (c) FOR CHILD OF DIVORCED SERVICE MEMBER (Child in custody of person other than claimant)—(1) Certified or photostatic copies of receipts from custodian of child evidencing serviceman's contributions for support, and (2) Divorce decree, court support order or separation order; (d) FOR DEPENDENT PARENT—affidavits establishing that dependency.

Bring your Social Security Account Number Card. If you do not have one, apply at nearest Social Security Administration Office. If you have life insurance, bring a record of the insurance company's address and your policy number. Bring enough clean clothes for 3 days. Bring enough money to last 1 month for personal purchases.

This Local Board will furnish transportation, and meals and lodging when necessary, from the place of reporting to the induction station where you will be examined. If found qualified, you will be inducted into the Armed Forces. If found not qualified, return transportation and meals and lodging when necessary, will be furnished to the place of reporting.

You may be found not qualified for induction. Keep this in mind in arranging your affairs, to prevent any undue hardship if you are not inducted. If employed, inform your employer of this possibility. Your employer can then be prepared to continue your employment if you are not inducted. To protect your right to return to your job if you are not inducted, you must report for work as soon as possible after the completion of your induction examination. You may jeopardize your reemployment rights if you do not report for work at the beginning of your next regularly scheduled working period after you have returned to your place of employment.

Willful failure to report at the place and hour of the day named in this Order subjects the violator to fine and imprisonment. Bring this Order with you when you report.

If you are so far from your own local board that reporting in compliance with this Order will be a serious hardship, go immediately to any local board and make written request for transfer of your delivery for induction, taking this Order with you.

SSS Form 252 (Revised 4-28-61)   (Previous printings may be used until exhausted.)   U.S. GOVERNMENT PRINTING OFFICE: 1965 O—769—162

My induction notice—such a nice welcome to the Army.

My basic training photo—what a fun time.

2

Flying to Vietnam on a Pink Jet

You just remember some things more than others, and flying to Vietnam on a pink jet just stands out in my memory.

After my last leave, I had to report to Fort Lewis at Seattle, Washington, for assignments and transportation to Vietnam. Earlier in the war, many people went over on boats, and often it would be entire units and their equipment all going together. By the time I went, there were five hundred fifty thousand Americans in Vietnam, so that meant there were thousands of soldiers rotating in and out of Vietnam every week. Since everyone was going by air, this called for a large number of passenger aircraft. The government was leasing airplanes from anybody that could provide them.

Does anyone remember Braniff Airlines? They were an air carrier that came up with a way to differentiate themselves from all other companies. They painted their planes different colors—chartreuse, aqua, yellow, and pink among other colors.

My fellow travelers and I got put on a *pink* jet to go to war. My thought was that when we got within sight of the coastline of Vietnam, the VC and NVA would look and say, "Well, look who they are sending to fight us now—their pink battalion."

First Helicopter Ride in Vietnam

I had flown on Hueys a few times in training back in the States, but my first ride in Vietnam was very different. It was more like an initiation than a training flight like they told us it was going to be.

I was told we were going to fly to a safe area and practice how to get on and off a Huey the Air Cav way. That sounded good to me; I wanted to do things the right way. We were flying along when things changed dramatically. The Huey felt and sounded like it was losing power suddenly. It turned out to be a controlled fall called auto rotation. The pilots practice this in case a combat situation causes a loss of power. The rotor blades keep spinning and the pilots still have enough control to keep it from being a complete free fall or a super hard landing. Got it?

Well, nobody told me they were about to do this, and I was sure my time as a living person in Vietnam would be very short. They reengaged the power and flew us to an area to practice our exits and entrances in a Huey.

The pilots and crew got a big chuckle out of this. They were lucky I didn't shoot them.

4

The Blues

Blues is a term you will see several times in the following pieces. The Blues are what we in the infantry platoon assigned to BlueGhost F Troop Eighth Cavalry were called. My call sign on the radio was "Blue 32" as leader of the second squad. Our platoon leader was simply "Blue."

An infantry platoon is ideally made up of four squads to total around forty men. We never had more than three squads, and if we got to twenty-five or twenty-six guys, that was a high point. Attrition due to deaths, wounds (physical and mental), and slow arrival of new replacements kept us low in numbers all of my tour. By far the largest percentage of the Blues were like me, draftees. There were some who had joined; we kinda wondered about them.

Now I will talk about my squad in the Blues and what we carried. One man (usually one of the bigger guys) toted an M-60 machine gun, which is a belt-fed automatic weapon that is fairly heavy. He also hauled as much belted ammo as he could stand. One soldier had an M-79 grenade launcher. This weapon looked like a short, fat shotgun, and it fired a projectile that looked like a short fat bullet but it actually was a small grenade. When fired, the trajectory of the round had a loop to it. My guy could put a round right where it needed to go. The ability of the M-79 handlers was amazing.

The rest of the squad carried M-16s. That is the clip-fed automatic rifle that fired a 5.56 mm round. The casing part of the round was large in comparison to the bullet, and there was a lot of powder to push the bullets out at great velocity. Earlier in the war, there was a jamming problem with the M-16, but during my tour, I didn't see much of that, thank goodness.

We all hauled a lot of other stuff. There were lots of pockets in jungle fatigues to hold M-16 clips, and we always filled them up. Several people would wear extra belts of M-60 ammo to be sure the machine gunner had all he wanted. In a fight, an M-60 is a difference maker. When the gunner opens up, an enemy has got to be very determined to hang in there in the face of that. Also, regarding the M-60, someone would always carry an extra barrel because the original barrel would get so hot it would droop.

We all carried canteens, grenades of various kinds, knives, side arms, bayonets, and wore steel helmets when we went on the ground. As a squad leader, I had an aluminum-frame rucksack that held a PRC-25 radio. On this rucksack, I hung additional grenades and extra water along with first aid materials. There was a belt and what looked like big suspenders called web gear. This web gear had attachments and loops that held my compass and more grenades at chest height. Around the belt were pouches that mainly held M-16 ammo clips. each clip held eighteen rounds.

You will learn more about the Blues as you take in more about BlueGhost and how it operated in its entirety. We were a part of an awesome machine when we headed to war.

The Blues went on the ground on search-and-destroy missions, and our other primary function was to get out downed air crews when we could. On one hand, we had it better than the soldiers in what we called line units. They would be out in the jungle for three or four weeks at a time. We slept in a bed most nights.

The other side of the coin is that they went long stretches with no contact, and we could be sitting around and the mission alarm would sound and here we go. Mount up, fly out, and be engaging the enemy in twenty minutes. We did that quite a lot.

In this whole writing, I will note, several times, the unbelievable youth of this group and how they performed. Never, and I mean never, did I see anything you could call cowardice or shirking of duty. That's not to say there wasn't an occasional dumbass moment, but that's going to happen in all walks of life.

When I look back and reflect on these guys, it always inspires respect and awe. Every man has to look in the mirror every day. Former Blues from F Troop Eighth Cavalry can look themselves in the eye and know they did their job and be proud of that fact.

It wasn't for sissies.

Blues making ready to go to war.

Helms, York, me, Gravino, Snider.

SSG. Harris (me) as Platoom Sergeant of the Blues.

5

Lift

These were the pilots and crew that flew the Hueys that transported the Blues on all of our missions. As stated in my section about Cobra pilots, I hate to try to give credit by name for fear of unintended omission. These fellows were highly thought of by the Blues and we owe them a lot.

Flying us out on a mission was no big deal if the LZ was cold with no enemy fire. The big deal came when the LZ was hot with enemy fire as we went in. Adrenaline starts pumping out your ears; the door gunners are firing M-60s over the Blues' heads as they are getting off and onto the ground. Those pilots had to hold steady as all this was happening. Stop for a minute and put yourself in a Huey pilot's position. Could you do it?

The next situation that made the Blues admire the Lift pilots and crews so much was that they would come and get us no matter what was going on. In the previous paragraph, I talked about a hot LZ going in. Imagine a hot LZ getting out. Sometimes the Blues would be on the ground and make contact with the enemy, and it would turn into a serious fight. The Loach would be firing at the bad guys and the Cobras have made runs on them. It becomes obvious the Blues need to get out of there. An LZ would be designated, and the Blues would move toward it.

The Lift folks have been flying overhead and listening to all the radio chatter down below. It's time to go extract the Blues, and they damn well know the situation they are flying into is more than hot.

The Blues pop smoke grenades, and the pilots acknowledge the color and head for that spot. Again the Huey glides in, stops, and hovers while the Blues get on. This takes longer than exiting. They head out and up with the Cobras firing on both sides to try to keep the enemies heads down. Both door gunners are shooting at targets of opportunity. Again, could you do that?

To say we were happy to see those Lift guys coming to get us out of those situations would be an understatement. Here though, I must say the saw cuts both ways. As stated elsewhere in these pieces, one of the things the Blues did was go in and try and save downed pilots.

I have seen the look in a pilot's eyes when he sees us (the Blues) coming to retrieve him from his downed helicopter. We knew the pilots would put their lives on the line to come get us, and we would literally go through hell and high water to get them back to safety.

There are so many incidents I could describe that exemplified BlueGhost Lift pilots' skill and courage. Let me tell you about this one.

We had been on a mission and completed it. We were heading back to Chu Lai when a message came in that said a long-range reconnaissance patrol (LRRP) was in dire trouble and had to be extracted immediately. The pilot was told we were the closest aircraft to their position and to go–Now. He informed them he had a load of infantry already on board and should he fly to an LZ to off load us as he had done in a previous situation like this. He was told no—there was no time.

He flew on toward the LRRPs, and since I had been listening to all the communication, I turned to my guys and yelled about what was happening and where we were going. We started down wind and we got ready to pull these troops on board as soon as they got close enough.

These men came running toward the ship, two on one side and two on the other. I was sitting on the deck in the door and I grabbed them by the web gear and pulled hard as they dove in. You could hear the pitch sound of the main rotor change; we were seriously overloaded.

We had come in on the crest of a ridge, and it continued straight out in front of the helicopter and it sloped off and down on both sides. Normally, a Huey stays in the direction it was going when it glided in. Conditions in front of him and the serious overload kept him from going forward. As I said, the ridge sloped down to the right and left. He chose to go left and that was the side I was sitting on. His maneuver of gliding sideways down the hill until we could get enough air speed let him turn the nose forward and we got out of there. Simple as that. The pilot was nineteen.

A quick addition to this account. As I said, I was sitting on the deck on the left side when we went gliding down the hill. Right in front of me was an NVA. He was startled to see the helicopter coming his way as he fell back on his butt to keep the skid from hitting him in the head. We both could have shot each other, but didn't. Things happen fast. I still think I would recognize that guy if I saw him today.

Two Hueys headed toward "Who knows what."

6

Cobras

Cobras were amazing machines for their time or any time. They were about the same length as a Huey, and the rotor blade was approximately the same as the Huey, but the body was about forty-two inches wide at its widest. When they rolled in to fire, they didn't present much of a target to shoot back at. They were also fast and very maneuverable.

Don't forget, I'm telling this from my perspective as a Blue. Cobra pilots are crazy. Maybe that's a little harsh, but not much. These were people, as most pilots were, guys who joined the Army so they could fly. Never mind that there was a war going on. They got to fly in max conditions—enemy fire, bad weather, good weather, and anything in between, they got to fly.

In another section I discussed armaments on a Cobra, and they are formidable. The electrically fired mini gun could put out six thousand rounds per minute. The grenade launcher was belt-fed, and the rockets were fired individually or could be fired all together. The rockets were of varying capabilities. The ones I remember the most were called HEs or high explosives. They would blow on contact, sending out shrapnel, and trust me, they were loud. WPs or white phosphorus (also called Willey Pete or Wilson Pickett) would explode, sending out pieces of white phosphorus, and if this stuff got on a body part, it would burn through until it fell out the other side. The sight of Willey Pete exploding is actually beautiful, but the results were rough. The last rocket style I'll tell you about is flachett rounds. They fired out from the Cobra for a specific distance, then they would explode again, sending out little steel arrows to rain down on the target. You can imagine what it would be like to be on the receiving end.

The Blues liked having Cobras close by when we were on the ground. It was like having an artillery unit at our disposal. This brings to mind one of the most important things I had to do as a squad leader and later as a platoon sergeant. We had to mark our position on the ground when it came time for the Cobras to shoot. This was done by putting out smoke grenades at both ends of our line and having the pilots verify those colors. Sometimes, another smoke was put out to mark which way was front. We then wanted them to make their runs parallel to our lines. Any confusion about this could be disastrous.

When Cobras started to work, the sound was otherworldly. There are some things you hear in war that will never be replicated, and these are some of them. The whoosh of rockets as they left the tubes, the blast of sound as they exploded, the *thump, thump, thump* of the grenades, and the loud whirr, like a huge sewing machine, as the mini guns fired.

There was another sound that only someone on the ground could hear. After the Cobras had made their run and pulled out, it would get relatively quiet, and there would be a tinkling noise overhead. The only thing remotely similar is a metal wind chime. The sound was coming from the brass shell cases ejected from the mini gun. They would be fluttering down and clinking against each other. Very often they would land in the water or a rice paddy and make another sound like throwing hands full of gravel into a lake. Never really heard anything since that truly represents those sounds, and I guess, I don't really want to.

BlueGhost Cobra pilots saw a lot of action. They not only flew with us but they were also often in support of other units in the Americal Division. Several were shot down. Some were wounded and some died.

I could call names of specific pilots and specific acts, but I'm afraid I'd omit someone. Suffice to say, from a Blues viewpoint, I was impressed with their bravery and skill. Once I saw a Cobra go straight at a fifty-caliber machine gun that was firing tracers right in the face of the Cobra. The Cobra finished the run and his wing man, the second Cobra, made the same run. The first Cobra swung around like a mad hornet and came at the gun again. The machine gun quit firing.

Two Cobras at a forward special forces base waiting on the call.

A Chinook sent to recover Bob Wiggins' Cobra after he was shot down.

Scouts

Previously, I had mentioned that Cobra pilots were a little crazy. Members of the Scouts were *way* crazy. This includes the pilots and the gunners. Keep in mind this is coming from the perspective of a squad leader in the Blues.

A friend from BlueGhost that I still see periodically was a gunner on a light observation helicopter. His name is Joe Loadholtes, and Joe sat in a little seat in the gunner position on a Loach. He had an M-60 machine gun hanging on a bungee cord and a big container of belted M-60 ammo. He is a tall fellow, and when he mounted the Loach, about the only thing inside was his butt. His arms, head, and feet were essentially outside and over the skid. We said it was kind of like a spider with a machine gun. From this position, Joe had one hundred and fifty-four confirmed kills. A whole volume could be written about Joe's time in Vietnam in the F Troop Eighth Cavalry Scouts.

I once told Joe that I thought he was crazy for doing what he did, and I wouldn't do it for all the tea in China. He responded that he would have nothing to do with the Blues because we were nuts for jumping out of Hueys and going on the ground. I guess it's all in your perspective.

The truth is, the Scouts had the highest percentage rate of deaths and casualties in all of BlueGhost. The reason is simple: they did very dangerous stuff. In another piece, I outlined the makeup of a BlueGhost mission team and that a Scout helicopter was down low at about treetop level.

Here, let me tell you a little about a Loach. They are very small helicopters with two seats in the very front for two pilots or a pilot and an observer. They are surrounded by a plastic bubble. The gunner has a small seat on the side. These machines are generally quiet compared to Hueys and Cobras.

As I said, they would fly at or below treetops, and even I was surprised when the Blues were on the ground to see them appear so quickly and quietly. If they were coming from behind a big stand of trees and then popped over the trees and dropped down, it was almost like they materialized out of nowhere. I know they were the last surprise that a lot of the enemy ever saw on this earth.

As the name implies, they scouted. From my perch at three thousand feet, I could look down and see a Scout ship scurrying around over the area in which we were about to do a combat assault (CA). Also, through my flight helmet, I could hear the info coming from the Scouts. They would say if they saw any cave or tunnel opening, hooches, or bunkers. They would note if the trails looked recently used or the grass or bushes had been recently disturbed. They were not afraid to say, "This just doesn't look right." Their experience in looking things over saved BlueGhost a lot of grief.

Scouts are the reason most of our combat assaults were cold, at least initially. They would have looked things over and not let us fly into a full-scale ambush. After we moved out looking for things, well, that's another story.

Again, from my perspective, the Scouts saved our bacon by being on the job and alert on a couple of situations that were similar. The Blues had been inserted, and we moved out to check out some hooches and bunkers some distance from the LZ. In both instances, we started to find maps, papers, and rice—lots of rice. There was enough to feed a couple of farmers for a year, so you knew the mouths it was intended to feed were close by.

There were two squads of Blues, a total of fourteen men on the ground. That is not a big-enough force to stand and fight for too long if you are outnumbered. We started to take sporadic sniper fire, which, by the way, will get your attention. About this time, the Scout started to say very emphatically that the Blues needed to get back to the extraction site. He said, "They are coming out of everywhere." As I remember, the verbiage was almost identical in both instances.

The Blues made I guess what you would call a fighting retreat to get back to the LZs in both cases. We lost one Blue KIA in one of the events and a door gunner on a Huey that came in to pick us up was KIA in the other event.

In both instances, the Scouts were alert and on the job. They more than likely saved us from a catastrophe.

I will forever be grateful and stand in awe at the bravery and professionalism of the Scouts.

Joe Loadholtes dressed to go to work.

Yes, there are tigers in Vietnam.
The villagers ask us to kill it because it ate several children.

8

How We Went to War BlueGhost Style

F Troop Eighth Cavalry had several different components. In this narrative, I want to elaborate on some of them. We had headquarters (command), supply, mess (food service), avionics (communication), maintenance, and other support personnel. All the functions were extremely important to any success we had.

As I have stated about all my writing in these pieces, it is being told from the point of view of an infantryman in an air calvary unit. Others had different views and perspectives based on their experience. This view is mine. It may be skewed somewhat by an attitude I acquired as time progressed. If you ain't Cav, you ain't sh——t!

With this settled, I'll move on to the basics of how we functioned. In the opening paragraph, I noted several of the pieces that made up BlueGhost. Now I will talk about the other parts. First, and the part I was assigned to, is the Blues. The Blues were an infantry platoon that put our boots on the ground when the situation called for it. We would be flown in on prearranged missions, and we would go down on search-and-destroy missions. Another function was to react to the downing of aircraft where we would try to secure the crew and save the aircraft if possible. Sometimes these adventures were called combat assaults (CAs) or insertions. I will elaborate more on this later.

The team that usually assembled when we went out on a BlueGhost mission were two squads of Blues flown out by two Huey helicopters. Then there would be two Cobra gunships and one light observation helicopter.

The guys manning the Hueys were called Lift. There were two pilots and two door gunners, with one of the gunners also being the crew chief. There were two pilots flying in each Cobra. One controlled the flight and the other the weapons. Their group was called weapons or guns. The fourth component was called Scouts and this was one Loach with two pilots and one gunner.

Once we arrived over the destination, the Hueys would make circles at about three thousand feet in the air. The Scout helicopter would already be down about treetop level, moving around looking to find the enemy or signs of his activity. The Cobras would be close by ready to react.

I, as a Blues squad leader, would put on a flight helmet as soon as we left our base. This had a cord to plug in to a jack in the ceiling of the Huey so that I could listen to all the chatter between the aircraft and I could communicate with the on board crew. When the decision was made and communicated to me that we were going in, I would remove the flight helmet and put on my steel helmet. I would then yell (it was loud in there) to my guys, "Lock and load!" If there was any other info, like bad guys to the left, I would yell that too.

We would start the glide toward our intended landing zone. This is called (long down wind). We, in the Blues, had a different technique for getting out of a Huey than you will see watching most films of Vietnam.

The BlueGhost style involved us stepping out on to the skids at about three hundred feet off the ground. One hand held on to the Huey and the other hand held an M-16 while both feet were on the skids. When we got close enough to the ground to know the jump wouldn't hurt, we jumped. The idea behind this was that if it was a hot LZ, meaning the enemy was shooting, you didn't want him to get lined up on you. Also, the Huey needed to get out of there as soon as possible. A Huey pilot hovering with nothing but clear plastic in front of him was like putting a sign on his chest, saying, "Shoot me."

Once we got on the ground, we would move out toward our assigned mission. The Scout would be flying fairly close by looking for anything and everything. The Cobras were on station ready to react with usually thirty-four rockets of various kinds, a nose-mounted electrically fired machine gun, and a belt-fed grenade launcher. Cobras could truly bring hell on earth.

That gives you an idea of how we were organized and how we got from point A, being a base of operations, to point B, usually being enemy territory.

Once on the ground, I never knew what would happen or how things would play out.

Blues skying up.

Me in my flight helmet along with Jim Snider.

Joe Loadholtes in the shooting position.

9

Combat Assault Vietnam Style

I got to Vietnam as an infantryman. I got assigned to a cavalry outfit and looked around but saw no horses. I learned pretty quick that my horse would fly. Also, I found out that our horses would take us from the fort out to the enemy a lot faster than Custer ever dreamed.

Combat assaults were heart rate boosters. I always called out, "Lock and load." We stood on the Huey's skids at about three hundred feet off the ground as the chopper glided into the LZ. When the jump was survivable, we jumped. Don't let the bad guys get ya lined up.

This was similar to the landing craft headed into a beach in WWII. You never knew what would happen when the ramp fell down.

CAs in Vietnam for a Cav unit were too numerous to count. Mostly, LZs were cold at first (no fire). Sometimes they were hot and adrenaline flows out your ears.

One time after a cold LZ, we moved out for a short distance, and Sergeant Linker put up his fist in the universal sign for halt. He turned his head, and in a low voice, he said, "I can smell 'em."

Mr. Fear ran through my gut wearing track shoes.

Am I going to finish out this year?

They were there all right.

Combat-A Primer

From my point of view, this is why many people say they understand combat, but they don't really. Sometimes you will hear athletic events described in terms of combat, saying, "We slaughtered them today," "my players fought hard," "we beat their brains out," or "we battled in the trenches today."

I know what they mean by this kind of talk, but the big difference is that all games are set up in a time frame and you can call time out or go have a conference on the mound when things start to get dicey.

Combat doesn't let you look to the official or umpire and call time out or say, "I need to talk this over with the coach."

Combat is strange in that, if you have the advantage or the upper hand, it's not bad. It is a jolt at first, but then your training kicks in and you take care of business.

On the other hand, when things go south right at the start, you realize that General Sherman was right when he said, "War is hell." It's bad to awful, and then it gets worse. You're thinking "God, give me a break, let me catch my breath, let me think." None of that is allowed—then it gets worse.

Out in the bush.
Foreground is me on the left and Paul Ratcliff on the right.
Behind us is Norman Gravino.

11

First Deaths

During Basic Training, AIT and NCO school, death is talked about a lot. Mainly how to prevent your own death and how to cause it in your enemies. It is always in the back of your mind. After all, the Army is there to kill people and break things.

My arrival in Vietnam was on my birthday, August 30, 1969. The airfield at Cam Ranh Bay was a busy place, but as I was walking down the exit steps, a baggage hauler came by pulling several carts, one attached to the other. It took me a minute to register that they were stacked with metal coffins being taken to a plane to be shipped home as freight. Happy birthday to me.

Eventually, I got through in country orientation and assignment to the Americal Division and then F Troop Eighth Cavalry. My specific job in the Blues started, and I thought, "This is not so bad." We went for a while with no significant action and no causalities.

My first encounter with a dead enemy was courtesy of a Cobra gunship. They had caught some NVA in the open and killed a couple of them. The Blues were inserted to "explore the situation," as the Army says. We soon determined that any live enemy had kept running and didn't seem to still be in the area as a threat. We turned our attention to the two dead guys. We were taught to check them for anything that could provide intelligence. After that, the soldiers did what all soldiers do since time began. We took their stuff.

If weapons are found, of course you take those. After that, it's a hunt for anything of value. In real terms or as a souvenir. I relieved one of these guys of his hammock. It was short but it worked.

It struck me as to how unaffected I was by seeing these people seriously shot up and dead. By then I had heard all the stories about what these guys had done to Americans. Summary execution on the battlefield, skinning live prisoners, beheading, testicle amputation, and other atrocities. I like to think I'm a nice guy and I was raised right, but there was no sympathy in me for them. My nice guy changed when we went down to a helicopter crash where it had been shot down. Seeing an American lifeless, broken, and burned shook me to my core, and that never changed during my whole tour. There were too many Americans I witnessed in many manifestations of death, and it got to the point that I would not look directly at them unless I had to. There's not much more I chose to say about this. It still hurts.

12

Just a Bunch of Kids

As I sit here writing this, I have to note that my seventieth birthday was one month ago. My God, how did this happen?

When it comes to age and time, sitting here writing these recollections, I marvel most at the age we were during our time as BlueGhost. My arrival in Vietnam was on my twenty-second birthday.

When I made it up to the American and BlueGhost and spent some time talking to folks it was a revelation to me that many of the pilots were only a few years older than me. Some were my age and some were younger.

Getting back to the premise of these writings, these are stories from my viewpoint as a Blues squad leader. The age of the Blues floored me. Practically all these kids were younger than me. When I sit here, now as an old fart, and look at the eighteen, nineteen, twenty, and twenty-one-year-olds that I know now, it stretches credibility to believe they could survive what the Blues of 1969 did.

Maybe I'm full of mud. Maybe I'm prejudice in favor of my age group, but the "kids" in my Blues squad did some fantastic things. There aren't enough adjectives to describe properly what these "kids" did.

Me enjoying the sunshine at 22 years old.
Chu Lai, Vietnam. 1969

Monsoon

I have heard the word *monsoon* in movies about India and China, but didn't think I would get to experience it in person. Just another one of the perks of getting sent to Vietnam.

For anyone reading this that doesn't know what a monsoon is, it's an extended period of nonstop rain. Sometimes it rains hard, and other times it diminishes to steady rain or an intense mist.

F Troop Eighth Cavalry was affected in that the weather didn't allow for much flying. As infantrymen, the Blues were okay with that,. Since most of us were draftees, we were not as gung ho as some of the career types. Not a criticism, just a fact.

Chu Lai, the main base of the Americal Division, is located in the northern part of what used to be South Vietnam. The monsoon that came every year lasted about a month or a little more. Two things I remember most about the monsoon season was that it was dreary with a capital D and *nothing* got dry. Everything was moldy, musty, and rusty.

When I look back, I realize that we had it pretty good during monsoon season compared to infantry units working out in the jungle doing foot patrols and night ambushes.

One monsoon in my lifetime is plenty.

14

My Fall into an Artillery Hole

You live and you learn. This was driven home to me on my very first adventure on the ground in Vietnam. We got word back in Chu Lai (the Americal Division base camp) that we were going out on a combat assault mission to an area where there had been a lot of NVA activity.

I had recently arrived in Vietnam, and on top of that, I was a newly minted noncommissioned officer. The squad I was installed to lead only had one other new guy, and the rest had been there for varying lengths of time. All of them had seen the elephant (meaning they had been in combat). Wanting to impress these guys that I was a capable and dependable squad leader was very important to me. You only get one chance to make a first impression.

We flew out and got on ground, which was an area covered with rice paddies in all directions. We started to move, and I had maybe taken ten steps in this rice paddy when my right foot went into a hole and I spun to the right and fell backward into a hole full of water.

There was a rucksack on my back holding a radio, C-rations, water, and extra grenades. I was wearing a web belt with more grenades, M-16 ammo, and more water; pant and shirt pockets were full of M-16 clips, and I had on a steel helmet. Plus, I was holding my M-16. Don't ever lose your rifle.

Here I was like a turtle on his back with my feet sticking up out of the water. The platoon members, I am sure, were looking at me and saying, "So this is another one of our great leaders."

The situation started to change for me from embarrassment to panic as I could not even start to get up. The more I struggled, the deeper I sank. That drowning in a rice paddy would be my end started to flash in my mind.

The guys took pity on me and dragged my near-dead carcass out of the hole. The water poured out of my helmet. My M-16 was held up, and water spilled out of the barrel. The expression "drowned rat" comes to mind.

When you look across a rice paddy, there are shoots of green rice sticking up in rows. One of the sergeants, another squad leader, looked me over and decided we could move out. But first he said to me, "Dumbass, when you scan a rice paddy and there is a perfect circle with no rice sticking up, an artillery round has landed there. Don't step in it."

Like I said, live and learn.

15

Old Lifers

There is a big difference between old lifers and career soldiers. Career soldiers are, for the most part, very good people whether they were enlisted or officers. Lifers are held in less regard. The acronym for L-I-F-E-R is Loafing Incompetent Fool Expecting Retirement.

In BlueGhost, we had three senior NCOs that captured the essence of lifers. None of us in the infantry could figure out what these guys did and how they kept busy doing nothing. Two were in supply in some fashion, and the other was actually assigned to the Blues when I first arrived. He was gone after a while back to the States, but he never went out on any missions. His ability to "skate" around responsibility was a marvel to behold.

My prejudice as a drafted infantryman may be showing up here. If you look at the Army as a big spear, the handle, which is support people, makes up 90 percent of the spear. The spear head is the combat arms, and out at the very point is the infantry.

BlueGhosts had plenty of people in combat positions—pilots, gunners, crewman, etc., but the guys who jumped off and put their feet on the ground were infantry. Every time we were inserted in those jungles, it was either you kill them or they kill you. Pretty simple, and the large percentage of these people were draftees. We were taking care of some very serious business that our country asked us to do.

When you are doing that kind of work under those conditions, it can't help but build a resentment toward those you know are skating or, even worse, those who are laughing up their sleeve at the cannon fodder.

16

Joe and I Build a Hooch

Joe DeLong and I were living at the NCO hooch in little compart-ments for each of us when I first got to F Troop. They were not much more than a place for a cot and a locker. After a while, we noticed an area on the back of the building where an addition could be added if the materials were available. They needed more compart-ments for incoming people, so we convinced First Sergeant Smith that we could build an extension on the end that would house us. He went along and got timbers, plywood, roof metal, nails, hand saws, hammers, and the equipment that we would need. We scrounged up everything else that we had to have.

Our plan was very basic, but it did turn out bigger than any-one suspected. The sleeping area accommodated two beds, two full-height lockers, a small refrigerator, and a small TV. Yes, there was one TV channel broadcast by AFVN (Armed Forces Vietnam Network). The luxury item that this addition had was a deck facing the South China Sea. We were the envy of everyone in the NCO hooch. We had a couple of chairs out there, and I put up a hammock I had taken off a dead NVA. Trouble was, those people were short and my feet hung over the edge.

Joe somehow came up with a four-by-eight piece of plexiglass. I got some hinges off rocket boxes, and we commenced to build a picture window that would prop open facing the ocean. We sawed the plexiglass in half lengthwise and attached the hinges in the top and hung those things side by side long ways. We had a sixteen-foot-long picture window, and we got some screen wire so we could prop it open and catch the ocean breeze without the mosquitoes.

Like I said, we were the envy of everyone. I think First Sergeant Smith would have moved us out and himself in if we hadn't built the place. It was a nice perk when you consider the situation, but we were forever being brought down to earth. The horn would go off, and we would grab our gear, get on a Huey, and be wading in a rice paddy in twenty minutes.

Joe got wounded and sent home. When I reached the end of my tour, there was a scramble among those NCOs remaining as to who would get the plywood Taj Mahal.

Me standing on the deck of the plywood Taj Mahal.

17

Leeches, Mosquitoes, and Snakes

Leeches are weird-looking little critters that live in water and will latch on to skin and suck blood until they are full. In Vietnam, I didn't encounter them too often, but you learned not to rip them off quickly. This would cause a worse wound. We carried a little container strapped to the side of our helmets that I called bug juice. It was primarily mosquito repellent, and if you squirted it on a leech, he would flop around and fall off.

Mosquitoes were a true bother. Number one, they could give you malaria, and one of my jobs as squad a leader and platoon sergeant was to remind my guys to take their malaria pills. Mosquitoes did something else to you. They made you sleep with a mosquito net over your bunk. This I had seen in movies before but never guessed I'd have to do it.

Mosquitoes bothered me most by the buzzing, droning sound they made. Some of them sounded like a small aircraft trying to land. One of the great exaggerations I heard was that "that mosquito was so big he could stand flat footed and have sex with a big dog."

Snakes are something I've never been fond of. During my in-country orientation at Cam Ranh, they showed us pictures of all kinds of venomous snakes that were common in Vietnam. They also showed photos of snake bites on soldiers' bodies. The wounds caused by these snake bites were horrific. After you saw that presentation, you were scared to put your foot on the ground. The bad part was that some of the snakes that could cause the most damage were little. Boots always got a turn up and a shake before putting them on.

18

Flares

Flares don't seem like the most exciting topic, but let me assure you, if you need light to illuminate an area where you are thinking that there may be someone who wants to kill you, flares become very exciting.

Flares that I became associated with were of two styles. Elsewhere in these narratives, mention has been made that our infantry squads rotated every third night to be at F Troop Eighth Calvary BlueGhost's forward base at Tam Ky. As described, this was a small airfield with a control bunker and some guard bunkers surrounded by perimeter wire.

During the day, Tam Ky was okay. There was the small town of Tam Ky to the south, highway one was to the east, and an old Marine camp to the north. To the west was flatlands and the mountains in the distance. There was usually a good bit of activity with BlueGhost flights coming and going, other unit's aircraft, and sometimes Air America (the spooks). As I said, during the day, it was okay, because you could *see* everything.

Then night falls and everything changes. You look at everything very intently at dusk so that you have every bunker, building, and tree located in your mind. Your best intentions to mark all these items in your mind goes out the window when it becomes full dark. You are a big, tough soldier in Vietnam, but you have to stifle the urge to call out "I want my mama."

Another thing I need to mention at this time is that you know the enemy is out there all the time. The question becomes, is he five miles away or five meters outside the wire?

I hope I have conveyed how interesting the transition from daylight to dark can be in an active war zone. Hence, the need for flares.

The flares we used most were round aluminum tubes about two inches in diameter and fifteen to eighteen inches long. They had an aluminum cap on the top end covering the tube top about two or three inches down. To fire the flare, you simply took the cap off the top and put it on the bottom. Holding the flare in one hand and pointing it where you want it to go, you then hit the cap with the other hand. It took off like a Roman candle.

These things shot up pretty high and then started to burn, illuminating a very large area. They stayed lit quite a while and floated down hanging under a parachute. There is no way to know the individual cost of these flares, but I can assure you my squad cost the taxpayers thousands of dollars in expended flares. You could have built a large circus tent with the material in the parachutes we sent fluttering to earth with our flare launchers.

The smaller flares we used were called trip flares. These were securely tied to something and then a trip wire was pulled across an area where someone might be walking that should not be there. The line would be pulled fairly taut a few inches above the ground. If someone came along and hit the wire, it would pull a pin and the flare would light up the world. Frankly, we didn't employ these a whole lot. They were most useful close to the opening of our main bunker. The opening was too close for us to put out an explosive booby trap, but the trip flare would warn us inside and temporarily night blind anyone who shouldn't be there.

Another flare that was fascinating to see was a huge flare pushed out of a plane at high altitude. It would float under a huge parachute and light up the night like day for miles around. We would watch these and know that somebody out on one of the mountaintop LZs was in a big fight.

These flares saved a lot of Americans and surprised the enemy who had been moving in the dark and all of a sudden was lit up like Christmas.

19

Serenading the Natives

This probably sounds like a weird title for a topic, but everything about this particular adventure appeared to me to be exactly that—weird.

The idea was to take a convoy by truck out to an LZ named Siberia. It got its name from the fact that its location was far out at the western edge of the Americal Division's area of operation (AO). This convoy hauled some supplies, but the most interesting freight it hauled was the Americal Division Band. The band was to play for villagers in that area.

F Troop Eighth Cavalry BlueGhost was tasked with flying cover over the convoy. This involved Cobras and Scouts flying low over the trucks to discourage any ambushes or pot shots. We in the Blues were high overhead in Hueys in order to respond if anybody got shot down. We just kept circling over and over, drilling holes in the sky. Kind of boring really.

"Pacification" and "win their hearts and minds" were big topics at the time. The geniuses at division headquarters decided to show the natives and the enemy how secure the route to Siberia was. The convoy was to motor out there, deliver the supplies, serenade the natives, and motor back. Sounds simple.

The trek out took much longer than they expected, and the enemy was uncooperative in that they blew a huge hole in the road at about its halfway point.

Well, the boys in the band got to spend the night, unexpectedly, at LZ Siberia. A night in which the enemy was successful in blowing two more holes in the road. Keep in mind this was no super highway. It was a dirt road barely wide enough for the trucks to pass. They had to bring in road graders and a lot of security so the road graders could work. The convoy got underway, and they finally got back to Chu Lai.

I wonder just how much the natives and the enemy were impressed.

20

The First Time I Saw Napalm

Just about everyone who has seen video footage of war has seen Napalm being dropped on a piece of ground. That was the case with me, but nothing, I mean nothing, will get your senses ready for what happens when this stuff hits the ground.

The Blues had already been in a dust up with what seemed like a small force of the enemy. They had withdrawn and that was fine with me. The Cobras shot at them a bit, but the Cobras had used up a fair amount of their ordinance already.

The Scout spotted even more bad guys in the area to where the original enemy troops had withdrawn. The decision was made for us to hold where we were. There was an F-4 in the area with Napalm on board. We marked our line with smoke, and the BlueGhost mission commander coordinated with the fast mover.

It sounded and looked like hell was opening up. The roar was deafening as the F-4 came down and then there was the sight of the canisters flipping over as they fell and the sight of the Napalm igniting. There was a fireball that is really indescribable and one thing I did not expect to see. The trees and big bushes around the perimeter of the fire got whiplashed inward due to all the oxygen in the area getting sucked into the fire. I'll just say that the aftermath of that stuff was grisly.

There was another use for a substance called Foo Gas. I really don't know if it was the same as Napalm, but if not, it was close. It was used in our area around the perimeter of LZs as a defensive weapon. Containers of this stuff were put out beyond the defensive wire, and it could be detonated remotely.

If defenders were being probed or they thought they were about to be attacked, they could set this Foo Gas off. It would illuminate everything and everybody. It would fry anyone unfortunate enough to be close by.

21

Touching the Devil

The Blues had been out on a mission that had its share of high-tension moments. We were very glad to be back putting our feet on the ground at Chu Lai. The job description of the Blues can be summed up by a definition I heard years after my return home. It was long periods of boredom interrupted by a few minutes of sheer terror.

As we moved off the BlueGhost pad, there was an assembly area that had a main rotor blade arranged as a bench. I sat down, and one of the Blues sat next to me. He said, "Sergeant Harris, we touched the devil out there today, and he let us go." He got up and walked back toward the hooches.

For the life of me, I can't remember his name, but I'll never forget what he said.

22

Bob Hope

The only two people outside of my family and friends that I shed a tear upon their death was Ronald Reagan and Bob Hope. Two great men in their own ways.

This regards Mr. Hope. As most of you probably know, he was a great comedian and an even greater patriot. He was tireless and unstoppable in entertaining soldiers, sailors, marines, and any others who happened to be around. He started doing this in World War II and did it in all United States-involved conflicts right up until a few years before his passing.

As stated several times in these writings, the Americal Division base was a big place. As such, it was on the list of places for the Bob Hope show to visit during Christmas of 1969.

I am sure lots of you have seen the spectacle of a Bob Hope show on TV. There would be thousands of happy faces laughing and smiling, pretty women singing and dancing, and old Bob telling jokes and funny stories.

Well, guess who was *not* at the Bob Hope Christmas show of 1969 at Chu Lai? It was me and most of the Blues along with Huey pilots, Cobra pilots, and their crews who were out flying in circles over the far perimeter of the Americal Division base. This was so that those fine, upstanding fellas with the jobs in the rear could enjoy the show without being bothered by the mean old enemy.

We were out there straining our eyes trying to detect any rocket or mortar activity that might disrupt their show.

I'm not bitter.

23

Back Page of the *Stars and Stripes*

The *Stars and Stripes* was a military publication that went out all around the world. It covered a variety of subjects. We were always glad to get reading material of most any kind.

The significance of the back page of the *Stars and Stripes* was that was where the list of dead from the previous weeks' action were listed. It was a macabre curiosity that drove me to scroll down those list. Too many times, I would find the name of someone from back home, someone from basic training, or someone from AIT (Advanced Individual Training).

The guys I had gone to NCO school with were also present on this list. We took some grief and we were called "shake and bake" NCOs because we made rank so fast, but it was those guys leading platoons and being in the action. They were way too much represented on the KIA list, and frankly after seeing their names so often, it made me think about the odds on my mortality.

The man who was my drill sergeant at Fort Benning had his name posted, and three of the four NCO cadre for my AIT group showed up before I left the States. That means they had to be killed within the first three months of their tour.

Seeing a name I knew on the back page was always like a kick in the stomach. It drove home the fact that my situation was more than real and I did not want to die. Their stories had essentially ended, and I wanted mine to go on.

24

Arc Light at Night

F Troop Eighth Calvary did a thing every now and then called a BDA—Bomb Damage Assessment. This involved flying out to an area that was on the receiving end of a B-52 bombing. B-52s flew from Guam or some other airbases in the Far East, and they would drop their bombs on a predetermined location. They would be at a very high altitude when the bombs were released, and then they would turn around and go home. These bombing attacks were called Arc Light Missions.

Somebody had to go out and see if they hit their target and, if so, what they got. Hence, the BDA. When flying over the effects of these raids, it looked like a large giant had gone through the jungle wearing round shoes. The look on the ground was no less spectacular. Of course there was a big hole. The dimension of these holes depended on the composition of the earth in the immediate area.

The holes would fill with water very quickly, and the area around the holes would be sheared off to dirt level for many meters with the grass and tree trunks getting progressively longer the farther you got from the center. When the distance was far enough for the wood structure of a tree to survive, the leaves would be blown off.

The mission of a BDA was to see what they got. There was actually a little sympathy, but not much, for the people that got caught in these drops. Sometimes, there would be pieces of fabric and smears of pink. You have to admit, it would be a quick way to go.

The reasons these bombings by B-52s were called an arc light was because of the spectacular show they put on at night. As these bombs started to hit the ground, the first to impact would explode, then the others would move across the horizon at the speed the jet was flying when they let the bombs go. It was a sight you can only see in time of war, as many of the things a soldier sees are in that category.

Another "war only" sight is Spooky shooting at night. Spooky was the designation for a prop-driven aircraft that was outfitted with many fifty-caliber machine guns, all shooting out of openings on the same side of the plane. The aircraft would identify the target area and then fly a circle over the target banking hard to the left. The weapons would all fire at one time with every fifth round being a tracer that glows red. It would look like a sheet of fire headed to the ground. Before the first rounds hit the ground, the plane would stop firing, and it did look like a red flying carpet flying into the ground.

A round would hit the ground every few inches when spooky attacked. Lord, have mercy on those caught in it.

25

Letters and Packages

One of the better times in Vietnam, or any war for that matter, was when the mail arrived and I got a letter. Nineteen sixty-nine and seventy were well before cell phones, instant satellite connections, and other technologies we take for granted today. The written word and cassette or reel to reel tape were the chief ways of communicating.

Letters from family and friends sort of drew you back into the world you left behind. Reading these letters was a time I would want to be left alone so I could withdraw into the picture painted by the words. When a letter was finished, coming back to the reality of where I was kinda brought me down.

All in all, letters were such a wonderful pick-me-up, and thinking about that, even now, makes me appreciate those who took the time and effort to write. Also, those who sent pictures really did my soul good. The old saying a picture is worth a thousand words is true.

Now packages are a whole different thing. I never got a package that didn't draw a crowd. I had some relatives that were good cookie bakers, and it was an unwritten law that you had to share cookies. The taste of cookies from "the world" was heavenly. A Sunday school class from the church where I grew up sent a package of assorted goodies. I still remember that.

26

Medevac Pad Placement

At the main base at Chu Lai, F Troop Eighth Cavalry shared a large area called a pad with a helicopter medevac unit. The area was fairly large and was covered with steel interlocking planking. Our aircraft parked on part of the pad, and the medevac unit took up the remainder. Just in case you didn't know, medevac helicopters flew out to retrieve wounded soldiers and also bring back the dead on occasion.

An Americal Division morgue was a short distance from the medevac area. It was really a big refrigerated box with big drawers. The dead would be placed there for a short time until shipment home could be arranged.

The flight way between our unit and theirs was shared. That meant we would taxi out and then take off looking over their area. Sometimes, not real often, they would be off loading dead guys to be taken to the morgue or KIAs (Killed in Action) would be lying at the edge of the pad in a row. This was not the best sendoff you could get when headed out to a combat mission.

You tried to shake it off, but those fellas had been as alive as me a few hours before, and like me, I'm certain they were sure it would be somebody else.

27

Mom and My Death

Thank goodness, my death did not happen in Vietnam. That's an easy point for those of us who survived on which to agree.

Going back to the fact that, in BlueGhost, I was a squad leader in an air cavalry infantry platoon, my odds of cashing in were higher than most.

After being there a while, it became very clear I could get killed doing this stuff. The finality of that thought was scary at first, but eventually, I would say, "Well, if it's over, it's over," and I wouldn't be worried anymore. It surely varied for different people as to what they worried about on that front.

My biggest concern was what my death would do to my mom. My wife would be hurt, but she was young, good looking, and smart. It would be tough, but I was realistic in looking at her situation. My daughter was an infant—she would make it.

Four years before I got to Vietnam, my younger sister had died with Cystic Fibrosis at age eight. My little sister was, without a doubt, one of the finest human beings ever put on earth. She was smart, sweet, and kindhearted. She suffered greatly from the disease but always was positive, and she had that little smile for everyone. She was the poster child for the Georgia Chapter of the Cystic Fibrosis Foundation.

Our whole community had taken her to heart, and at her funeral, the church was overflowing. Grief overcame the whole place, and there was sobbing, crying, and moaning that was uncomprehendable.

In a nutshell, I just did not want Mom to go through that again.

28

NVA Aid Station

There was a spotting by a Loach of a suspicious setup. We were inserted close by to go in and check it out. The Scout had seen human activity and observed some people going into an opening in a bunker. They had also seen something they could not quite figure out. So being the accommodating guys that we were, the Blues jumped in to try and answer their questions.

When we got to the bunker, it looked like two bunkers close together. We heard scurrying around inside the opening, and since we had a Vietnamese scout on the ground with us, he told them to come out. They did not. He yelled again. Still no response. This kept up for a while, and then they were told that if they did not come out, grenades were coming in. Still they refused.

Two concussion grenades were thrown into the bunker. These things are loud with a capital L. No one came out. The scout spoke again, and in a minute, a frag grenade went in.

Finally, there were spoken words and people started to come out. Three women and a man emerged. The assumption, from their appearance, was that they were medical personnel. This was confirmed by all the medical material we pulled from that hole and the medical setup they had in the two bunkers. These prisoners were taken to be guarded while we surveyed the rest of the site.

What caught our eye, and the eye of the scout overhead, was their system for getting water from up on top of the hill to down where they were.

Let me try to explain this system. Picture a triangle laying on the ground with each leg of the triangle being four feet long and made of bamboo. Now take the triangle by one of its three points and lift it up ninety degrees. The point in your hand will be the highest point with two legs sloping down and away from your hand. The third leg will be resting on the ground. Now visualize about forty of these six feet apart going up the face of a gently sloping hill.

Now get twenty pieces of bamboo six feet long. Cut them in half long-wise; now you have forty pieces that are shaped like little troughs. Now place the end of one of these troughs on the point of the first triangle and place its other end on the point of the second triangle and tie in place with bamboo strips. Repeat putting troughs on top of triangles all the way down the hill.

A long piece of bamboo ran from a spring at the top of the hill to the start of the viaduct. It was sort of like the Romans. It got fresh, clean water to where it was needed. We were impressed.

The prisoners were moved closer to the pickup area so they could be taken to be interrogated. The Vietnamese scout who was with us was a Chu Hoi scout. That meant he was a former NVA soldier or Vietcong (VC) who had come over to the South Vietnamese side. They sent these Chu Hoi scouts to work with American units as guides and interpreters.

The prisoners were told to stand up and move toward the helicopter, and as they came to their feet, the Chu Hoi scout walked over in front of the male prisoner and shot him from about two feet away. When I say shot him, I mean he emptied a whole clip from an M-16. We were shocked and dumbfounded. The women prisoners freaked out.

We were pointing weapons at the scout because we didn't know what this guy might do. He acted nonchalant and lit a cigarette and acted like it was another day at the office.

Everyone was eventually loaded up and flown out of there. Reports were written but I never heard the outcome.

29

Rocket Box Construction

I never knew the exact dimensions of a rocket box. They were made of a lighter grade of wood. They were about forty-eight inches long by ten to twelve inches high and fifteen to eighteen inches wide. The top was hinged, and I believe they had rope handles on each end.

The name rocket box derived from the fact that the rockets fired by our Cobra gunships were transported from the States to their point of use in these boxes. Once the rockets were removed, the boxes were set aside to be used in various ways.

The chief way I saw them used was in what I call rocket box construction. The lid would be opened, then the box was filled with sand, and then the top would be secured down. These sand-filled boxes would be stacked like bricks to form substantial structures. The main building, the control tower and our guard bunkers at Tam Ky were made in this way. They could absorb a pretty heavy impact, and they would definitely stop a bullet.

The wood in these boxes was very high quality. Wood to the Vietnamese was especially valuable because the whole area of the flat lowlands had been stripped of any significant timber years ago.

At the height of the monsoon season, the water around Tam Ky kept rising and rising. It got so high that one of the guard bunkers at the airfield's end was cut off. Our guys couldn't get to the bunker so they spent the night at the main building and control tower. When the sun came up, the bunker was gone. The civilians in Tam Ky had negotiated chest-deep water and razor wire to get the wood.

I was impressed.

30

Security for a Downed Mail Plane

This account was told to me by a member of the Blues that was on this mission. I've told you that the Blues were tasked with recovering downed crews and downed aircraft. This usually meant helicopters, but one time, the Blues were flown to the site of a C-123 fixed-wing cargo plane that was designated for carrying mail. It had crashed on a coastal river, and it was pretty unclear as far as enemy activity was concerned. It was sketchy enough that they wanted the Blues around to secure a perimeter so that the Graves Registration people could go in and retrieve the bodies. Isn't that an interesting name for an Army department—Graves Registration?

I guess their job was okay when it was just paperwork back in the rear, but when they had to go in on situations like crash sites, I didn't envy them at all. The Blues had no problem that day. The enemy didn't show as there were Cobras circling around and around overhead.

The Blues position was fairly close, and the retrieval was grisly as they got those fellows out. The plane had hit pretty hard apparently, and Graves Registration pulled out two bodies that had been under water for a while.

The Blues never heard if any other crew members survived. You can bet those guys never thought they were going to die in Vietnam. They had a cool job, flying a mail route.

31

Tam Ky Shuttle and Shrapnel in a Fire Barrel

Tam Ky was a town north-northwest of Chu Lai. Chu Lai was on the coast by the South China Sea, and it was the main base of the Americal Division, of which F Troop was a part. The F Troop main base was there, and it housed practically all the F/8 people. As a member of the Blues platoon, we had hooches there, and we flew out of there most of the time.

There was a forward base manned by BlueGhosts at Tam Ky. It consisted of a PSP (portable steel planking) runway that could accommodate small- to moderate-size airplanes and any kind of helicopter. There also was a control tower and sleeping area made of rocket boxes filled with sand. There were guard bunkers around the airfield with razor wire fencing around the whole place. A fuel blivit was also placed at the Tam Ky field so that choppers did not have to fly all the way back to Chu Lai to refuel. A blivit is like a big flat balloon filled with jet fuel.

The Blues (infantry) platoon usually consisted of three squads. A Blues squad had to man Tam Ky, so every third night, my squad would be at Tam Ky. You ate C-rations, drank warm water, and wondered what the hell was going on out there in the dark beyond the wire.

One night in the small hours of the morning, there was a tremendous explosion. An enemy rocket had hit the runway at the far end. At sun up, we saw a hole in the runway, and the PSP was bent up and out around the hole.

At the time of the impact, it was pitch-black, and we could not see what had happened and we were on high alert expecting an attack. After the explosion, it got deathly quiet. The only thing I could hear sounded like someone taking a whiz, you know that stream of water hitting the ground. Who the hell is doing that at a time like this?

Soon, the whizzer was found. A fire barrel (fifty-five–gallon drum filled with water) had taken a hit from a piece of shrapnel from the explosion. The barrel was about one hundred fifty yards from the impact. It brought to mind stories I heard from other wars how people were killed by small pieces of shrapnel from faraway explosions.

I'm just glad none of my guys got punctured. The next day, another squad got shuttled in, and we went out on a mission before we were taken back to Chu Lai.

Me standing by where a rocket impacted the runway at Tam Ky.

*Me with fire barrel at Tam Ky
that got a hole in it from shrapnel.*

The flight control tower at Tam Ky.

32

A Mother's Love

This account was told to me and I feel compelled to write about it here even though BlueGhost were not involved.

Two friends of mine got drafted and ended up in the same unit in Vietnam, and one of those fellows was killed while the other made it home.

The soldier who survived knew the family of the soldier who died. The survivor went to visit the family, and of course, they wanted to know what happened when the KIA occurred. He filled them in and they thanked him. Next, they told him what happened on this side of the world on the day of the KIA.

The mother and the sister were living together. The sister said her mother got agitated and yelled, "Your brother just called out to me," and then she insisted they needed to contact the Red Cross. The mother said if they hadn't heard something by the next morning, they would contact the Army. They got word the next day of her son's death in Vietnam.

Later, sometime after the funeral, the sister got the exact time of her brother's death in Vietnam. She then correlated it to what time it would be in the Eastern Time Zone of the United States where they lived. This time lined up exactly with when her mother heard her son call to her.

The reason I include this is to say there are things that are simply beyond comprehension. Trying to figure out something like this will leave you frustrated, so don't. Just accept that the love between a mother and her son is in a realm that leaves us to marvel.

33

Calm Chatter

As a squad leader and later Platoon Sergeant of the Blues, I noted that I put on a flight helmet every time we got on a Huey. This allowed me to listen to all the chatter within my Huey's crew and communications among other aircraft involved in that mission. When the Blues went on the ground, a PRC-25 radio was in the rucksack I carried with a wire running to a speaker attached to my steel helmet right over my ear.

The reason I'm telling you this is so you will know I listened to a heck of a lot of talk. Every now and then, I would talk with folks flying overhead, and there was the infantry platoon's internal communication.

The point I'm getting to is in combat, you might expect people to get overly excited in the way they converse. Surprisingly, this was rare. The most inspiring and amazing to me was the way the pilots would talk as they were literally getting shot down. They would say "We are taking fire," and a few seconds later "We are going down," and this was as calm as if they were calling their mother to say "Hi, Mom, how was your day?"

The situations would invariably get very hairy, but the consistency of cool demeanor was always there.

As we got on the ground and started to move, let me give you a little snippet as to how we communicated:

Blue 32: Blue, this is Blue 32. We have movement to our right.

(Blue was the platoon leader.)

(Blue 32 was me.)

Blue: Blue 32, this is Blue. How many and how far?

Blue 32: Blue, this is Blue 32. At least three or four at two hundred meters.

Blue: Roger that.

Blue 31: Blue, this is Blue 31. We just took fire from an AK-47.

(Blue 31 is the first squad leader.)

Blue: Blue 31, this is Blue. Where from and how far?

Blue 31: Blue, this is Blue 31. About the same spot Blue 32 saw.

Blue: Blue 31, this is Blue. Roger.

Blue: Blue 32, this is Blue. Hold in place.

Blue 32: Blue, this is Blue 32. Roger.

Blue: Blue 31, this is Blue. Hold in place.

Blue 31: Blue, this is Blue 31. Roger.

Blue: BlueGhost 26, this is Blue. We have contact. We will mark our position and give you distance and direction.

(BlueGhost 26 was a great Cobra pilot.)

BlueGhost 26: Blue, this is BlueGhost 26. Roger.

Blue: Blue 32, this is Blue. Mark the end of your line.

Blue 32: Blue, this is Blue 32. Roger.

Blue: Blue 31, this is Blue. Mark the end of your line.

Blue 31: Blue, this is Blue 31. Roger.

Blue 32: Blue, this is Blue 32. Smoke is out.

Blue 31: Blue, this is Blue 31. Smoke is out.

Blue: BlueGhost 26, this is Blue. Smoke is out. Identify.

BlueGhost 26: Blue, this is BlueGhost 26. I have banana yellow on one end and goofy grape on the other.

Blue: BlueGhost 26, this is Blue. Roger. From our position at 120 degrees and 200 meters is target.

BlueGhost 26: Blue, this is BlueGhost 26. We got 'em.

Blue: BlueGhost 26, this is Blue. Roger.

BlueGhost 26: Blue, this is BlueGhost 26. Tell you people to get their heads down. Coming hot.

This is a short sample of those conversations, and I hope it gives you a little better feel for the subject. The calmness of this was almost always stable and smooth. You would logically think otherwise, but no, calm is the word.

34

Armor Fight Northwest of Tam Ky

We were flying back from a mission that had been uneventful (the best kind), and everyone was feeling pretty good and happy to be getting back to Chu Lai for a hot supper and a shower later. As we got to an area northwest of Tam Ky at about dusk, I was surprised to look down and see tracers flying all around. Most of the tracers were red, but some were green (NVA). It became apparent that what we were looking down at was a fight between an American armored unit and the NVA. We could see the armored personnel carriers (APCs), tanks, and mortar tracked vehicles.

The Americans were putting out a lot of fire, but what got everyone's attention was how much fire the NVA was throwing out. Whenever the NVA chose to stand and fight rather than move away, you knew they were ready to fight it out.

I had on my flight helmet, which I always put on when we were in the air, and the chatter quickly got my attention because the higher-ups were trying to decide if they needed to put the Blues on the ground or not. They finally decided there would be no way to add fourteen infantrymen as reinforcements to a hot-armor fight. We weren't cowards, but we were relieved not to be set down in that one.

We were doing circles over this fight at about three thousand feet. I was amazed to watch medevac choppers (Hueys with the Red Cross) go flying in and land right behind the armored units. They would load the wounded and fly out with tracers flying all around them. As soon as one left, another would fly in. During my year in

Vietnam, I saw our BlueGhost pilots do some extraordinarily brave things, but these medevac pilots and crews took the cake.

During all this, I happened to be looking right at an armor vehicle when it blew to bits. I learned later that it was a track that had a mortar in it. It had a big round hole in the top for the mortar to shoot out. Apparently, an enemy mortar round went right in the opening and set off that horrible explosion. That whole crew was gone in an instant.

The battle kept going for a while longer, and several medevacs were in a holding pattern waiting their turn to go in and extract wounded. We had to leave because our fuel was getting low. Sometime later, I heard that the NVA broke off the fight and melted back into the jungle before it got full dark.

35

Division Guard Duty

Some weird things happened in Vietnam. My stint as Sergeant of the Guard for division guard duty was one of them.

As I have stated before, the Americal Division headquarters base was one big place. There was protective fencing all around the perimeter and tall guard towers periodically placed. These towers had structures on top that I called small hooches. Two guys were assigned there at night all the time.

F Troop Eighth Cavalry's main camp was inside this fencing along with thousands of other people. Well, the Army method of manning these towers was to pull sergeants from all the units, put them in a pool, and rotate the responsibility among them as Sergeant of the Guard. Well, my name came up, and I was told to report on a specific date and time to a numbered tower.

I showed up around dusk and climbed the ladder up to the hooch in the sky. It had a front room that looked out toward Highway 1 and the terrain adjacent to it. There was a door in the middle of the back wall that led to a little room with a cot in it. There was a fairly large building close to the foot of the tower. I would learn later that it was an officer's club.

When I got up there (and it was pretty high), I introduced myself and shook hands with these two guys. I was twenty-two and they looked like kids to me. As I said before, this was their full-time Army assignment. One was a private and the other a specialist.

They had land line connections to all the towers and the Officer of the Guard. There were some powerful lights they had the controls for and plenty of flares.

The main thing they had was some electronics I am sure they commandeered (stole) from somewhere. With this gear they had a speaker/receiver in the tower and the same speaker/receiver in the kitchen of the officers club. They also had rigged a rope-and-pulley system with a basket that could be raised and lowered to the ground.

After my introduction, a little small talk, and a very quick review of guard protocol, they politely said to me, "Sarge, you don't mess with us and we won't mess with you." I was taken back by this, but then I thought to myself, *I'm a draftee and I do my job in the Blues, but I'm not going to go all spit and polish on these guys.* This turned out to be one of my better decisions.

They did their job, a little squirrelly at times, but they checked in with command as they should and turned on the big lights every now and then. Before too long, once they decided I wasn't going to be a hard ass, they asked me what I wanted from the officer's club. Turns out they had developed friendships with the cooks down there. They lowered the basket and called on their speaker/receiver and told a cook to send up a list of what was available. Up comes this list, and I pick out shrimp and a rib sandwich. They "called in" the order and down goes the basket. Before too long, the speaker squawks, and they are told to pull up the basket. In the basket is one of the biggest shrimp cocktails you ever saw and a beautiful prime rib sandwich with a side of horseradish. Oh yeah, and they had added an ice-cold Coke. Later, was a vanilla ice cream snack.

I dozed most of the night on the cot in the little rear room. At one point, I asked through the door, "What was that smell?"

One of the guys replied, "Don't worry, Sarge. It's a Winston."

You have got to pick your spots when you go all spit and polish.

36

F-4 Crash on the Beach

The base at Chu Lai was big. There were two full Marine Air Wings flying missions out of there. It was said at the time that the busiest airport in the world was at Danang, about fifty miles up the coast. The second busiest was Chu Lai. The airbase was at the other end of the compound from us, and the only time you didn't hear the dull roar of jets was when helicopters were running up.

The kind of fighter jets that took off from there were F-4s. They normally flew in pairs. The volume of planes taking off and landing was remarkable, and you could watch as jets would be spiraling in the sky, stacked up waiting to land. As soon as one would land, another would take off and so on.

As I have noted, our troop area was right on the beach, within one hundred to two hundred yards. While walking in the troop area on a bright clear day, I heard a very loud roar and looked south down the beach to see two F-4s coming north. The plane on top had flames streaming behind it, and the other fighter had positioned himself so that his canopy was right under the plane that was on fire. They were trying to assess the situation and figure out what to do.

They decided the guy on fire should go up to some altitude and point his jet toward the South China Sea and he should punch out. That's what they did as I and several other people watched this happen. It was interesting to watch the pilot eject, and his chute deploy as he floated toward the ocean. A boat was speeding out to get him and was there about the time the pilot hit the water. This was fascinating to watch, and we were all relieved that a bad situation had concluded as well as it had.

Well, almost. We turned our attention to the jet headed out to sea to see it disappear in the distance as I'm sure the pilot had intended. That was not what happened. That thing started to climb and climb until it started to bend back and was upside down. Holding that same trajectory, it started coming back down.

Take your right hand and hold it flat facing away from you. Start moving it forward and up at an angle. Keep doing this and your hand will make the loop I described above.

My fellow soldiers and I had been taking all this in when it dawned on all of us at about the same time, "That damn thing is coming back." Everything was happening so fast that we got what I call happy feet. That plane was going to hit with a full load of bombs and fuel, and it was going to hit close. By the time I decided which way to run, it was over. It augured into the ground, going straight down at hundreds of miles an hour. It hit about one quarter to one half mile away about two hundred yards from the beach. Thank God no one was killed, but in a little bit of justice, the explosion knocked the commanding general's hooch off its foundation.

37

Gary Ista Gets Shot Down

The mission started out with a BlueGhost team headed toward a place that had picked up the name Death Valley. The beast was out there, and I could feel it in my bones. Call it intuition, precognizance or whatever you want, when you get "that feeling," you just hope the better angels are on your shoulder.

Two Hueys with two squads of Blues flew into a situation that I did not like from the start. We got on the ground, which was a rice paddy, and to the left was higher ground, in front was higher ground and to the right were tall, dense trees. The Hueys had to hover, turn around, and go out the way they came. Not good.

We moved to the left, got out of the paddy, and moved through a good bit of bushes to get to an area that held a few hooches. They all had bunkers under them. We spread out and started searching the bunkers. Almost immediately, we started pulling out paperwork, cooking paraphernalia, and a bunch of rice in big bags. If you have any sense at all, this will put you on 150 percent alert. No humans were to be seen.

About that time, a couple of sniper rounds zipped through where we were standing. Luckily, no one was hit, but then the fire increased a bit. We were getting ready for a fight.

I carried a PRC-25 radio in my rucksack on my back, and I had a cord running from it to a small speaker that clipped to my helmet right over my ear. The handset I could talk on hung on a clip ring on my web gear over my chest.

The speaker started to crackle with the information from the Scout that was flying over the side of the hill to our front. He said there were NVA coming out of tunnels up above us and NVA farther up the hill coming down our way. His most urgent advice was to get out of there and make our way back to where we had first landed. This sounded like a very good idea to me.

This was where I injured my back and survived one of my scariest episodes. As their fire was picking up, some rounds hit a tree right above my head. It was time for me to get down. I glanced at an opening to my left and perceived it to be a little drop off where I could at least get some cover and protection.

I went for this little drop, but as soon as I pushed through the bushes, it turned out to be about a six foot drop down to yet another rice paddy. My momentum propelled me to do a flip in the air and land on my back in rice paddy water. The force of landing on my rucksack holding the radio was terrific. I thought my back was broken because I couldn't feel or move my feet. I truly felt that the end of my line had been reached.

At this point, the NVA motivated me. I had sort of slid and pulled myself into a sitting position. Looking around, I could not see a single Blue. They moved toward the pickup area, and I was on the end of the line. An NVA heavy machine gun started putting rounds in the water to my front right, and as he swung the gun, the splashes headed my way. Recoil saved me because as he swung toward me, his shots went higher, and by the time he got to me, the shots hit in the bank over my head. As he swung further, they started to hit in the water again.

One of the BlueGhost Cobras had apparently seen him shooting and put rockets right at him. Don't know if he killed the shooter, but it made him stop shooting. My ass was motivated. I got up and moved as fast as I could to catch up with the rest of the Blues. Again, adrenaline is a magic elixir that your body generates for free. We arrived at the extraction point and had to slog through that damn mud and water in the rice paddy. It makes you move in slow motion when your mind is on the accelerator.

Those poor guys in the Hueys had to hold a steady hover while we got on board. My squad got on Tom McCone's bird, and the other squad mounted Gary Ista's ship. This put Gary in the lead and Tom behind him.

I was sitting on the left side of McCone's ship so I had a front row seat to what was about to happen. A machine gun about fifty to seventy-five meters to our left had started firing at the helicopter in the lead. The gun was later estimated to be a thirty-caliber machine gun. The rounds started to impact the tail boom and the tail rotor of Gary's ship. Pieces of the tail rotor were flying away.

I saw where the muzzle flashes and smoke of the machine gun were on the ground. My left hand was pounding on the leg of Bob Neal, the left side door gunner from Texas. I was pointing toward that gun. Bob was already on it, and he poured M-60 fire right on them. Thank God, he made them stop shooting because after hitting the first ship, the shooter would have swung on us and I was sitting facing them.

Looking toward the lead chopper I saw one of those scenes that is maybe my most vivid visual memory of the war. When a Huey loses its tail rotor, the whole body of the helicopter starts to spin around. The tail rotor is what keeps a helicopter flying straight.

Gary was, I'm guessing, two hundred feet or so off the ground when the tail rotor was shot away. As the whole thing started to spin and they headed for ground, things started to fly out of the sides from centrifugal force. Helmets, weapons, and anything loose, and sadly, a door gunner was ejected. He had a safety cord attached, but they tell me it was let all the way out. No matter, he grabbed the skid with his hands and held on all the way down. His feet were straight out from the force of the spin. He hit when the helicopter hit. The Huey had landed on its skids, and then it bounced once and came down on the door gunner's neck. I will never forget that series of events.

I am told by pilots in the know that Gary Ista's skill and guts saved that situation from being a whole lot worse. There is no doubt that Bob Neal's skill and nerve as a door gunner is paramount in saving our ship from disaster.

The Blues on the downed ship were lucky. They got banged up, bruises, broken bones, and they cut their fingers and hands holding on, but the door gunner was the only KIA.

This situation wasn't over. The Blues in my squad were landed as close as we could get to the crash. We formed a defensive cordon around the others as best we could with seven guys. We also tried to aid the others to the best of our ability. Keep in mind we had not gone far at all from the area where there were a lot of bad guys.

Medevacs came in to take out the KIA and the injured. That leaves seven of us on the ground, and thank goodness, our BlueGhost Cobra and Scouts were still overhead keeping the enemy at bay. My day had already been getting shot at by AK-47s, shot at by a heavy machine gun as I am sitting in rice paddy water, and then watching a ship full of my platoon mates get shot down right in front of me. Now my squad was back on the ground wondering what was going to happen next.

Next was information over my radio telling us to get ready for a Chinook (a very big double rotor helicopter) to arrive so they can hook up the downed Huey and haul it out. If maintenance couldn't make it flyable they would cannibalize it for parts.

This all sounds pretty straight forward and doable. I'd seen it done before. It took some time before the Chinook arrived and I was informed via radio that our BlueGhost coverage was going to have to leave and go back and refuel and rearm. The mission commander assured me that they had artillery and jets on standby if we needed them. As they flew off, it got quiet and I have to say that was unnerving. We all looked at each other with very wide eyes.

It wasn't too much longer until the Chinook arrived, and about that time, an F-4 jet flew in close overhead. As an infantryman, an F-4 on your side is a very, very good thing. They get the enemies attention. Napalm and high-explosive bombs are things to be universally feared.

A soldier called a rigger came down a rope from the Chinook, and his job was to rig a big nylon-and-steel fiber strap to the head of the Huey and then to an attachment under the belly of the Chinook. He also attached a fairly small parachute to the tail end of the Huey.

This chute was to fill with air as the Chinook with the Huey hanging under it started to move, thereby keeping the Huey's tail at the rear. Got that? It sounds doable.

In this case, it did not work. The reason was that due to the terrain, the Chinook could not just get the Huey off the ground and fly away. He had to hover and then go straight up for quite a ways before he could move laterally. No filling in the chute caused a huge problem.

The body of the Huey started to spin around slowly at first as the Chinook tried to lift the Huey up. In no time, the Huey is spinning very fast, and then it spun so fast I could not believe anything that big could spin that fast. It then became like a blur under the Chinook.

At first this was all interesting to see happening right in front of us. We had expected them to pick it up and be gone. Next it got alarming because I could see that the wild spinning of the Huey was causing the Chinook pilot to have trouble controlling his craft. He would slide to the left and back to the right, and when he swung to the right, he was on top of us. Next, it really got interesting.

Have you ever had one of those little balsam wood planes powered by a rubber band? You twirl the propeller around and around as it is attached to the rubber band in the body of the little plane. Get the band wound into a ball and then let it go and the propeller spins and the plane flies. Lots of energy in that balled-up rubber band.

The strap between the Huey and the Chinook started to ball up like that wound-up rubber band. The Huey was being pulled up toward the bottom of the Chinook, and the ball was getting bigger. Every time it would swing over us, we would jump around like cats on a hot tin roof.

I made a C in physics, but even I could figure out this wasn't going to go on much longer without a catastrophe. BlueGhost Six, our CO, had arrived overhead, and I was calling in my handset for them to get away from us. About that time, they swung away from us and the wound-up ball exploded into fragments and the Huey dropped. It hit on the edge of a big drop off. It appeared to quiver for a second then rolled over and over down that hillside. Later, an F-4 dropped ordinance on it to keep the enemy from getting anything.

At a reunion, I heard someone say that the Huey was flown out and salvaged. I'm sorry, that is incorrect. Norm Gravino was standing right beside me as we watched this happen—ask Norm.

A BlueGhost Huey came in to pick us up, and we were gone back to Chu Lai. What a day. By the way, I get a 20 percent disability rating for my back.

Gary Ista and his craft some time before the shoot down,

Me looking in to Ista's downed Huey.
Photo by William Patterson (A Blue)

38

Respect for the Enemy

Let me be clear as a bell on this subject. Communism is a terrible form of government, and it never works in the long run. The people it subjugates are stripped of practically every basic right that we enjoy. Soviet-style Communism imploded after around seventy years, and China altered its style to accommodate capitalistic sectors. The old guard in Hanoi has finally slid a little more toward the Chinese model.

At the outset, Ho Chi Minh was more of a nationalist than a pure communist, but he saw it as the horse to ride to achieve his goals. The man could speak to his people, and he could motivate them to great sacrifice and courage. The south never had any leaders like that.

My growing up years were formed by the Cold War and the ever-present real fear of nuclear annihilation. To say I didn't like communism would be an understatement.

Getting back to me as a squad leader in the Blues, I was smart enough to see that many aspects as to the prosecution of the war had not gone well, but now I was in Vietnam. It was time to put politics away and take care of the business at hand. The people we were assigned to fight fought under the banner of Communism so I had no hesitation in going after them.

I want to be clear again. I do not praise the enemy at all, but there came to be a respect for the tenacity and skill he displayed. If you did not acknowledge this, he would hand you your head.

In 1969, I did not want the communist to conquer the south, and when I watched on TV in the mid-seventies when Saigon fell, I felt physically ill. Also, I did not want Communism to expand anywhere else in the world.

Now as I look back as an infantryman in the American Army at the infantryman in the North Vietnamese Army, he may have finally defeated the South and united Vietnam, but he still got the booby prize—Communism.

39

Rodent Control NCO

Rodent Control Non-Commissioned Officer, it has a nice ring to it, doesn't it? Not really. It took no time after this assignment came my way that the platoon was nicknaming me Rat Man.

The Army, in its infinite wisdom, has charts and lists that must have assignments made to fill them in. I was not aware that there was a Rodent Control Officer and Rodent Control NCO in each unit. The officer got his notice and called me in to say, "Sergeant Harris, go forth and control rodents." He gave me some paperwork as official Department of the Army instructions, and I, in turn, selected some lucky platoon members to kill rats. There were some perks to being an NCO.

We learned some things about rat killing. If you poisoned them, they crawled under hooches where they died, rotted and stank. The temperature would make this situation almost unbearable. The other option was traps. The rats were so big I actually saw one hobbling around with a trap clamped to his front leg. We had just succeeded in making him mad. We got bigger traps and staked them by wire to corner posts at the edge of the hooches. When the traps sprang shut, the huge rats would flop around like a hooked bass. Eventually most would pull themselves free. Then they would go back farther under the hooch where they would die and stink. Rats always get revenge.

After a while, we made minimal attempts to bother the rats and things kind of settled into a delicate state of eco-equilibrium. The one plus of this whole situation was that I got a cool flight helmet out of the deal. David York, a member of the Blues, was quite a good artist, and he volunteered to paint my helmet. He placed this panicked-looking rat face on the back looking out with big bloodshot eyes. Everyone who saw it was impressed.

Sadly, I let someone borrow it and they neglected to snap the strap around the seat frame as I always did when going on the ground. It rolled out at some point and was lost. I wondered if some NVA or VC found that flight helmet and wondered just what kind of people he was up against.

40

Tien Phouc

Tien Phouc was a name I had heard discussed. From my limited information and understanding, it came across as a place that was out on the fringes of our area of operation. Green Berets and Rangers worked out of there and long-range reconnaissance patrols (LRRP) missions headed out from there toward the Laos border. This was an area I later came to call the Wild, Wild West.

Tien Phouc was a village down in a valley, which differentiated it from the many landing zones (LZs) we were more familiar with. LZs were on mountains or at least high hills. The tops were flattened out, and bunkers, artillery emplacements, and other structures were constructed. This was encircled by razor wire, barbed wire, booby-trapped explosives and claymore mines. The jungle outside there would be cut back to give the defenders clear fields of fire.

The LZs had some unique names: LZ East, Center, West, Gator, Professional, Fat City, Ross, Siberia, Hawk Hill, and Mary Ann.

One day we were told to get ready to go out to Tien Phouc and that we would land there and be ready to act as reinforcements if needed and be a recovery team if any of the BlueGhost aircraft and crews went down. Two Hueys with the Blues on board flew out with some Cobra gunships and light observation aircraft (Loaches).

We landed and the infantry guys got off the Hueys, and we found an area to sit down or lay down if the conditions of the ground and the insects allowed. After a while, I learned that infantrymen could fall asleep most anywhere that conditions were amenable.

We found ourselves at the edge of a small runway that didn't seem long enough or wide enough to be practical for planes to land or take off. Helicopters—yes, but planes—no. It wasn't long until I was proven wrong. A style of plane called a Caribou came into view, and it made a half loop overhead, glided down over the face of the mountain and landed with a few feet to spare at the end of the runway. I was impressed at the spectacular landing, but also concerned because we all heard the distinct sound of enemy rifle fire as he started his glide down the face of the mountain.

The pilot jumped out and looked at his aircraft to see if there were any hits. He looked over at everybody and made a safe sign like a baseball umpire. He turned to some guys who had run out to unload, and he urged them to "Get this sh——— out of there so I can get the hell out of here."

He got back in, and the unloaders picked up the back end of this plane and literally pushed it back into the bushes at the end of the runway. One of our pilots said that was because he would need every inch of runway to get out of there.

He revved that thing up then let off the brakes. He zipped down the runway and took off at a sharp angle, and he skimmed the tree-tops as he flew up the face of the mountain. Again, we heard the *pop, pop, pop* of an enemy weapon. The pilot won this round.

No sooner than this little bit of excitement had concluded, we heard a child screaming desperately. We went toward the sound and found a little fella who was scared to death and hurting. He had been playing beside a worn-out barrel from a huge artillery piece. The barrel had rolled onto the kid pinning him down. We got together and rolled the barrel off him and found that he was unharmed. When your job is all about killing the enemy, it felt good to save a child from harm.

No one needed reinforcements and no aircraft went down, so we basically spent the day sitting and sleeping for the most part. A LRRP team called in that they had found an American boot with a foot in it, but no body to be found. That was strange, but I was to encounter a whole list of strange things before my tour in Vietnam ended.

We loaded up and flew back to Chu Lai. The local enemy sniper did not shoot at us as we left because our Cobras were already up, and he knew if he exposed his position, the Cobras would unleash hell on his head. I always really liked Cobras.

My adventure at Tien Phouc was over and we never went back. I've never missed it one bit.

The Blues could sleep anywhere.
Snider, me and Helms

A Caribou at Tien Phuoc.
You have to see one of these take off to believe it.

Crappers and Burning

This is a delicate subject. It regards bodily functions and the disposal of the results of these bodily functions. We had outhouses for answering these calls of nature. Since our unit call sign was BlueGhost, we called our outhouses Casper's crappers.

These crappers were seldom one holers. Most of the time, they were communal with multiple seating opportunities. They were little buildings with a wood floor, walls, and a roof. The back of the building had a solid back for the upper half, but the bottom was a flap door that could be folded up and fastened. Inside under each seat was a fifty-five–gallon drum cut in half.

I will let you guess what was caught in these barrels. Upon reaching a certain point, the barrel had to be pulled out and a "clean" one inserted. Something had to be done with the full barrels. You just could not pour it on the ground.

The solution was to burn it. Diesel fuel was added to the mix and set on fire. This flamed up and burned down. After a while, it had to be stirred and more fuel added. This process continued until the contents were reduced to ashes.

Lucky individuals got assigned to this duty. It was "dooty duty." My assignments as rodent control NCO seemed glamorous compared to sanitation NCO.

I'm So Lonesome

We had USO shows from time to time in a maintenance hangar where a stage had been constructed. Most of these shows were Filipinos or Koreans; hardly ever did we see Americans. It was absolutely amazing how these groups and individuals could "knock off" American groups and individual singers.

One show that stands out in my memory was a young Korean man. He did a country-themed segment, and he was a marvel at how he could imitate people. His performance was upbeat and lively until he got to a point and he said, "Now I want to do a Hank Williams song." It got quiet in there and he started to sing:

> The silence of a falling star
> lights up a purple sky
> The moon just went behind a cloud
> to hide his face and cry
> And as I wonder where you are
> I'm so lonesome I could cry.

A lot of soldiers had to turn their heads and wipe their eyes. I was one of them. Go to Google and look up all the words to "I'm So Lonesome I Could Cry" then put yourself in our position in 1969.

43

Joe DeLong's Early Leap

The Blues raised getting off a Huey helicopter to an art form. When pilots and crews of a Huey would fly us to our destination, called a landing zone (LZ), we would exit as quickly as possible. This would involve us getting off our seats and standing on the skids at about three hundred feet off the ground. You held on to the Huey with one hand, and your weapon with the other hand.

When you felt the jump was survivable, you jumped. The whole idea behind this was to get on the ground ASAP so the enemy did not have time to line up their shots at the Blues or the chopper and its crew. While we disembarked, the Huey was essentially hanging still in midair. It felt like the pilots and gunners were attempting to remain calm and hoping not to get shot. They wanted to get back up to some altitude in a hurry. I think this describes the need for us to get unloaded quickly.

Well, Joe was a great solider, our Platoon Sergeant at the time, and a conscientious leader. He felt he should lead by example. We were flying out to do a combat assault at a designated site. We were gliding in on a downwind, and as we got closer, everyone moved to stand on the skids in preparation to jump to the ground.

Being the leader, Sergeant DeLong jumped from a height that I thought bordered on Superman crazy. Right as he jumped, the copilot started waving his arms and yelling to indicate not to jump. They wanted to off load us about thirty to forty meters farther ahead. Everybody else was still on board.

I looked back at Joe who was about hip deep in rice paddy water and mud. He had a stricken look on his face as we moved off. In my most-caring manner, I leaned out a little farther and waved goodbye.

He got me back "big time." He later got wounded by a piece of shrapnel in the back of the hand. It broke a little bone in his hand. When you get a broken bone of any kind and you are serving in the tropics, you get sent back to the States because of the fear of infection.

Joe didn't have very long to go to finish his Army obligation, and the Army was not going to send him back to Vietnam for a month. They gave him a medical discharge, and he was out of the Army and a civilian again.

Yours truly was still very much in the Army and still in Vietnam. By this time, I was Platoon Sergeant.

Joe sent a note to me, and in it he said when playing golf, his hand only twinges a little bit during his back swing.

44

Like an Old West Shoot-Out

Remember when we were kids and we would watch a western movie? The good guys wore white hats and the bad guys would wear black. They would jump up to shoot at each other then drop down to hide for a bit. They repeated this process several times, and they never reloaded their six shooters. Finally, the good guy would "wing" the bad guy and haul him off to jail.

Fast-forward to the early part of 1970 in Vietnam, and I found myself with the Blues flying out on yet another mission in the central part of I Corp West of LZ Hawk Hill. This was the main base of the 196th Light Infantry Brigade.

It started out as a standard BlueGhost operation. The Blues were inserted at the bottom of a hill, and we were instructed to move up and over a series of patty dikes to get to the top where some activity had been spotted. We were led this day by Sergeant Alvin Linker.

Before I go further in this narrative, I feel there should be some description of who Sergeant Linker was and what he did. He was the infantry soldier's infantry soldier. When he came to F Troop Eighth Calvary, he was on his third tour. He was about thirty-five or forty, and we considered him old. He had the CIB with two clusters (look it up). He had been under fire in Korea, the Dominican Republic, and Vietnam. Also, he had sat on an airfield in Florida with his jump gear on ready to jump into Cuba during the Cuban Missile Crisis.

Alvin despised the state-side Army, and he was born to fight and kill his enemies. I've already written about one day when he put up

98

his fist and said, "I can smell 'em," and he was right. Having him on your side was a true asset. Some people can shoot a basketball; some throw a baseball. Alvin could fight in combat and kill the enemy. Thank God.

As we got close to the top of the hill, Sergeant Linker was out front and to my left. Also out front and to my right, a guy popped up and took a shot at Linker then he dropped back in a bunker. I was moving, trying to get to a position where I might get a shot at the guy. Linker fired at him and dropped down. The enemy jumped up and shot again. The enemy concealed himself, and Linker came up and shot twice then he faked that he was going down. When Linker did this, the enemy started to rise and Linker shot him in the head. The enemy got fooled by Linker's fake. It was the last mistake he ever made.

We moved up toward the bunker, and Sergeant Linker was coming in from the left when someone came out of the bunker and took off running. They were wearing the black pajama outfit worn by the VC. Linker took aim and shot. It turned out to be a woman, but you had to look hard to tell. This was the second woman I had seen killed. The other was running out of a building from which we had taken fire, and my M-79 grenade launcher took a snap shot that hit her in the neck, taking off most of her head. Sincerely seeing them die did not bother me at the time because they would have gladly killed us if they could have.

Back to the shoot-out. When I made it up to the bunker, there was an SKS rifle laying by the dead guy and the back of his skull was gone. His brains were on the ground. The reason I mention this is because within a very short time, we started taking a good bit of fire, and I had to get down on the ground right next to this fellow's brains. The smell was like warm syrup, and I could not eat waffles or pancakes for years. Thankfully, I got past that. Also, I don't know who got the SKS rifle.

As I said, we started taking fire from the enemy and it got heavier. I was on the ground as were members of my squad in a line to my right. Felix Grajeda saw some enemy movement to our front and decided to throw a frag grenade at them. He pulled the pin and raised up to throw the grenade. It had not gone very far when it hit a tree dead center with a thunk. The grenade came flying straight back toward us. Luckily, there was a little rise in the ground right in front of us. The grenade stopped on that side of the hump. We hugged Mother Earth like never before, and that thing exploded. There is no way you can replicate the sound of a grenade exploding that close.

We had to make a fighting retreat from that place with the BlueGhost Cobra gunships shooting rockets and mini guns all around to keep them off of us.

We made it to an LZ back at the bottom of the hill and got picked up and flown out of there. What a day.

This picture was taken right after Sgt. Linker had won the shoot out.
Upper left is Felix Grageda. Lower right is me.
Photo by William Patterson (A Blue)

My Inane Notebook

Being a squad leader at first and then Platoon Sergeant had its serious moments, but it also had its day-to-day living that had to be taken care of. There were things that had to be done by me and other tasks the soldiers in the platoon had to accomplish.

I was looking through my memorabilia when considering writing these pieces, and there was my last notebook from Vietnam. The name inane notebook seemed to fit. That may be a misnomer because some of the notations had serious ramifications. My first note was as follows:

> Frags – 104
> White Phosphorous – 15
> Smoke – 35
> Concussion – 23
> Incendiary – 7

This, of course, was an inventory of the platoon's grenades. At first we got all the grenades we wanted, but after an attempt on the CO with explosives, he got a little jumpy, and we had to account for all explosives.

My note of April 28, 1970, said as follows:

1. Plain fatigues tomorrow
2. One man for guard duty

3. Leave the EM club if asked
4. Grace and Arnold for awards
5. 31.60 FM
6. Don't deal in MPC
7. Kramer, Lesperance, Borean – R&R
8. Trip flares

These are things I got from the First Sergeant and things my platoon leader may have passed along to me. As an example, I will elaborate on this list from April 28. We would have a formation and the info would be passed along.

1. The note about the fatigues was to tell everyone about which uniform to wear. Some were plain and others were camouflage.
2. We (our platoon) had to provide a person for guard duty.
3. There was an enlisted man's club—if you got drunk and they asked you to leave, you better leave.
4. Awards will be presented at troop formation.
5. 31.60 FM – The frequency of the day for our radios.
6. MPC – Military Payment Certificates. This was the form of our money in Vietnam. There was a black market for local currency and gold—don't do it.
7. R&R was *R*est and *R*ecuperation – Everyone got a week R&R during their tour. Destinations were all over the Far East including Australia and Hawaii.
8. Be sure to take a case of flares to Tam Ky.

These were notes from one day. I'll list some more so you will get a feel for all seemingly routine things that had to happen in addition to our main tasks, flying and fighting. This is a compilation of several days:

K.P Fund – $3.00
Awards at 1300 at 570th
No loaded weapons until I say lock and load

Conserve water
Haircuts
Nez – R&R in June
Don't knock down "No Swimming" signs
If you cancel R&R let the head shed know
Malaria test – nets must be up
Must take your white pill
Can take clothes off down to shorts 1700 to sundown
Don't mail restricted items – 2 yrs & $10,000.00
Stanley – get paid
Weapons inventory
Check bunkers
Always have dog tags
Sodas at Hawk Hill – 20 cents
Chow – 0430-0530 only
Max Ventilation – doors propped open

I hope you can see there was a lot going on. Some of it mundane and some not. We never seemed to finish one list before there would be another.

46

Allen Is Gone

The day I learned that Allen Caldwell had died was tough. A letter came from my wife telling me that she had gotten word that Allen had been killed in November of 1969. This letter was several months after the date; I had not seen him listed in *Stars and Stripes*. I did not get to see every issue, and there's no telling who else's death I never knew about.

There was mention of Allen in other sections of this writing. He was a fellow soldier I met in AIT, and then he, William Blanton, and I went to NCO school together; we were all drafted Georgia boys caught up in the war.

Upon completing NCO school, we got thirty days' leave before we reported to Ft. Lewis, Washington, for transfer to Vietnam. We got there together, but during the processing, we got separated, and William and Allen went one day ahead of me. They wound up in the same unit down south with the First Infantry Division (the Big Red One). My assignment sent me to the Americal Division and F Troop Eighth Cavalry BlueGhost. It turns out we did the same thing; they were also in an air cavalry unit.

Several years after the war, I finally located William, and this is where I learned the details about Allen's death and other incidents in William's tour. He was with Allen the day he was killed. William also told me what he knew of Allen's family. This led me to meet Kenny and later Bert, Allen's brothers. They are great people and they loved their brother dearly.

William told me of the fight the day Allen died. Their platoon had been put in to block a unit of NVA fleeing from a larger American force. The Americans had hit the NVA hard, and when they withdrew, the enemy soldiers ran into William and Allen's group. There were more NVA than anyone expected, and they ran through, around, and over Allen's group.

William said Allen was hit and died right away. William also said the fighting was so fierce that most of them ran out of ammo and were literally throwing rocks at the enemy. Then it was over. The surviving NVA moved on away.

I knew several people in BlueGhost that died and they all hurt, but for some reason, the notification of Allen's passing jolted me very hard. During NCO school, Allen, William, and I had talked about getting together after the war. We were "Georgia boys," and we liked each other and respected each other.

William Blanton and Allen Caldwell are the kind of guys that, if born in another time, would have performed their duty on Omaha Beach or Iwo Jima.

Back in greatest generation days, after some of those epic fights, people would marvel at the grit and sacrifice of those soldiers, sailors, and marines. The classic question was "Where do these people come from, and how does America produce them?"

Allen and William were produced by America, asked by America to serve, and they answered the bell. They didn't run away, dodge, or evade. They are the ones the greatest generation would be proud to call peers.

To this day, I still struggle with why Allen's passing bothers me so much; maybe it's because he was so respected by William and me. Maybe it's because after the war, I learned how much he meant to friends and family.

He is buried at the Post Cemetery at the entrance to Fort Benning. If you find yourself in that neck of the woods, go by and look up his location and say hello. Say more if you want to. Don't know how much it will help Allen, but you will be better for it.

47

Beaches, Sharks, and Bunkers

The South China Sea was the ocean view from our hooch at the F Troop Eighth Cavalry BlueGhost headquarters at Chu Lai. This was part of the main base for the Americal Division, which at the time had thirty-three thousand troops. Many of these troops were out at various landing zones. The bulk of support troops were at Chu Lai, which was like a fair-sized town—air fields, support buildings, housing, and a large hospital.

The beaches along this part of the coast were beautiful. They had sand comparable to Panama City, very white and it was almost blinding with the sun shining on it. The waves breaking on our part of the beach were usually big enough to create a nice sounding surf. It was very conducive to sleeping. This was one of the few perks of the situation. To knock the luster off this tropical scene were the guard bunkers and the concertina wire that was between our hooch and the beach.

I expected wire, bunkers, and tall guard stations on the side of the division headquarters to face inland. They were there, and there were many of them. The bunkers and wire facing the beach were necessary because the Vietcong had boats of all sizes, and they could land people under cover of night.

The reference to sharks resonates with me because I never saw any from my hooch, but when we took off over the ocean, there they were. There were plenty of them and they were big. Someone would drop a concussion grenade in the water, and the explosion would stun one and it would roll over with its belly shining. Quite a sight.

48

Opportunity to Re-Enlist

My friend Charles Wiggins was a machine gunner with the Blues, and he was in the squad of Sergeant Roger Caruthers. Charles is from Bladenboro, North Carolina, which is in Bladen County. This is important to this story later on.

The Blues had been tasked with trying to recover American bodies at the base of LZ West in August of 1969. It was a miserable, hot, and very dangerous assignment. This all happened prior to my arrival in Vietnam, and to be honest, I'm glad I missed it. This account was told to me by Charles, Roger, and others who were there. If you have further interest, read Keith Nolan's *Death Valley: The Summer Campaign of 1969.* This book is one of the best accounts of no-holds-barred warfare you will ever read.

Charles and the others were recovering the bodies of Americans killed several days prior to the arrival of the Blues at the base of the mountain on which sat LZ West at the top. It was August in Vietnam, and the temperature was over one hundred degrees most of the time, so you can imagine the state of the bodies they had to deal with.

Roger said they had fully loaded a Huey with bodies, and it was having trouble taking off because they have a harder time rising in extremely hot weather because of poor lift. This left the squad with no flight out and a need to get to the top of the mountain, so they started to climb. About this time, they also became aware the NVA was not too far behind them. The climb was steep, hot, and slick.

The guys said they would push one person up, and he would turn around and extend his M-16 down to pull up the next guy. They kept doing extraordinary things like this all the way up. Many of them threw away things that caused extra weight. Some had only part of their clothes and their M-16 at the top. Some didn't have that. By the way, the NVA had set fire to the grass below them. Roger said that one man had given up and told Roger to shoot him. About that time, some flying embers from the grass fire below landed on his bare skin and he got up and made it to the top of the mountain.

The people in LZ West were jumpy to say the least. They had been attacked the night before, and they had killed NVA in their perimeter. Bodies were hanging in the wire.

Roger said they wanted to make sure the Americans inside the LZ knew not to shoot them. He said someone in the wire challenged him, and he replied in his best east Tennessee accent, "Who in the hell do you know who talks like this?" They got in.

Now, back to Charles. Charles is one of these people who has a great sense of humor. When he walks in a room, you kind of smile. He has that effect.

Well, when he made it to LZ West, it was a relief. They spent the night, and it turned out the next day was the Army's day to talk to draftee Charles Wiggins about his opportunity to reenlist. They really do keep up with that closely. Turns out a First Sergeant and a Captain found Charles and another soldier and got them in a bunker to tell them about the advantages of re-enlistment.

Charles said he was polite and listened to their presentation, but when it was over, he told them, "If I ever get back to Bladen County, you will have to burn off the swamp and sift the ashes to find me."

49

Leadership

Leadership is a vital ingredient in a military unit that can make it flourish. Lack of leadership will make it flounder.

When I arrived at F Troop Eighth Cavalry BlueGhost and was assigned as a squad leader in the Blues platoon (infantry), the first introductions were to my acting Platoon Sergeant and the Platoon Leader.

The Platoon Sergeant was transferred out shortly after my arrival so I never got to know him. My first Platoon Leader was Skip Booher, but he also got rotated home shortly after I started. We never went out on a mission together, but he impressed me as capable. I heard complementary remarks about him from some of the old hands. Since the war, I've gotten to know Skip through our reunions and he is a fine man.

Dave Harrigan replaced Skip as Platoon Leader in early fall of '69, and it is Dave I want to primarily speak of in this piece. He had a unique start on life in Japan. His mother is Japanese and his biological father was American. This was right after the end of WWII, and his prospects were bleak because Japanese society is extremely tough on mixed-race children. Adopted by an American officer and his wife, he came to the United States and had an all-American childhood and was graduated from Texas A&M. He was commissioned a second lieutenant and made his way to Vietnam.

Dave came to F Troop after spending the first part of his tour down south as an infantry officer in the First Infantry Division. He had some experience when he came to us, and it was evident right off the bat that he was no rookie. Being inserted as the Blues platoon leader came right away, and there was no doubt who was in charge.

Leadership can be assigned, but in the real world, it has to be earned. Lt. Harrigan earned the respect of everyone in the Blues because he would not ask us to do anything he would not do himself. That sounds pretty simple and I guess it is, but Dave was consistent and operated this way all the time.

The Blues rotation system to Tam Ky meant that one squad was there every third night, and this left the other squads to fly missions for the Blues. This meant that, every third day, you generally got a day off from flying and going on the ground. Dave did not get any days off, so he flew all the time. Also, if the Blues were on the ground, he went with them whenever possible.

Dave had "it" whatever "it" is. He was fearless to the point of being careless with his own safety. He was never careless with his men. Their well-being was forever at the center of his thinking. All the Sergeants who were squad leaders would literally follow Dave anywhere.

Let me emphasize this point. There were plenty of officers in Vietnam who did not meet any of the things described in the previous paragraph. Going into combat with someone that is weak, careless, or both is a nightmare for the troops that have to follow them. The trouble was that you couldn't vote them out if you got stuck with a bad one. Those of us in the Blues were extremely lucky when Dave was assigned to F Troop.

Dave was in the thick of a lot of the Blues' more-serious actions. He was standing beside Roger Caruthers when Roger was shot; he was in the middle (literally) of the bad Cobra shot that was so awful. He won the Silver Star in an event that was reported to me by platoon members who were with him as this happened. They came to me as soon as they returned to Chu Lai, and they all said that what they had seen Dave do should be rewarded with the Congressional Medal of Honor. They were dead serious about this.

They said, "Sergeant Harris, you can write better than we can, so take this down and say it in a way we can take it to the commanding officer to start the process," In summary, this is how I remember what they told me.

A Loach had been knocked down and the enemy was very close by. The aircraft was on fire in the middle of an open area. Dave ran to the burning craft and pulled out all three crew members. One was already dead, one was alive but died later, and one survived. There was enemy fire during all of this. This is a very abbreviated description of what they told me, but it is as I remember it. The thing I recall most vividly is the determination these guys had for wanting Dave to be recognized for what he had done. They were in awe of what they had just witnessed.

Within a few days, Dave was awarded the Silver Star, which puts him in a very small fraternity of soldiers. Everyone was proud of Dave but felt the recognition should have been higher. Dave was twenty-three at the time of this event.

There are many ways to describe leadership, but I will say it here in a way I have said to many people over the years. If Dave Harrigan called me today and said, "John, you need to be in Seattle Sunday afternoon at three o'clock" and hung up the phone, I would start making arrangements to be in Seattle at three o'clock on Sunday, no questions asked.

What a leader looks like.
Dave Harrigan—"BLUE"

50

Friends from Home

When you are in the Army and literally half a world away, you don't expect to see people from your hometown. To have it happen is a real treat, and I was lucky enough to have it happen twice. Crazy as it may sound, basketball was the catalyst for both encounters.

I have talked about the location of F Troop Eighth Cavalry main base being in the huge Americal Division perimeter. Adjacent to BlueGhost's area was a flight maintenance battalion, and they had several big metal buildings with concrete floors. Learning that they had put up a basketball goal in one of the buildings close by F/8, I naturally would wander over during my down time and look for a pick-up game. People have certified me as a genuine basketball nut.

A game had started, and all of a sudden, someone called out, "Hey, you're Johnny Harris." It was Jerry Green.

Jerry was from Fairburn, Georgia, and we had gone to the same high school, Campbell of Fairburn. He was a little younger than me and had joined the Army and gotten into helicopter maintenance. It was great to see him, and we saw each other from time to time mostly shooting hoops in that metal building.

I knew several of Jerry's relatives, and he knew a whole lot of mine. It gave us plenty of things to think about. It's so nice to see someone from home when you are so far away and in that situation.

The next guy from home was another Johnny; his name was Johnny Routon. We had been on the same basketball team at Campbell; Johnny was a senior, and I was a junior during the 1963–

64 season. We went 22 and 3 that year and were ranked number one in the state most of that year.

Johnny Routon was a great teammate and a good person. I mean good to the bone. He had the gift of making all who were around feel comfortable, yet he could take control and lead when the situation called for it.

Johnny had been in the Army for a while unknown to me when I got drafted. He had gone to OCS (Officer Candidate School) and had gotten a commission as an artillery officer. By the time he came to see me in Vietnam, he was a Captain.

This is an aside, but I had to include this at this point. Years later, I spotted a bumper sticker that said, "Artillery – We Bring Order to What Otherwise Would Have Been an Unruly Brawl."

We were landing at Chu Lai when I looked out and said, "Damn, that's Johnny Routon." Sure enough, it was him. He was in the Americal Division and had learned that I was there and where I was located. He took the time and made the effort (it's not easy traveling around a war zone for personal reasons) to come see me.

I was flabbergasted and so happy to see him. We spent about half a day reminiscing and catching up on people back home. We also talked of our current jobs in the Army and how all that was going. It still brings a smile when I think about that time.

Here I must admit that it didn't really register with me at the time what an effort Johnny had made to come visit me. Recently, Johnny died, and it was finally realized by my feeble mind what a truly special thing he had done all those years ago.

Thanks, Johnny. Rest in peace, dear friend.

51

Hoe Handle

Joe Delong was a platoon sergeant and I was a squad leader at the time of this incident. This is one of those "you had to be there stories."

The Blues had been inserted at the bottom of a small hill. We were to move up to an area that had been recently plowed. Routinely, when we were on the ground, we would be in radio conversation among the squad leaders, the platoon sergeant, and the platoon leader. In addition, there would be talk with the helicopters overhead. Most of the time, the communications were necessary and to the point; sometimes, they would be inane or someone talking just to hear their own voice.

Well, we moved uphill and crested a little rise. In front of us was a small plot that had freshly turned dirt. There was a hoe in the middle and footprints of the recently departed farmer.

About this time, the radio came alive and someone flying overhead said to Joe, "What do you see and how long do you think they have been gone?"

He immediately answered, "I don't know how long they have been gone, but this hoe handle is still quivering." Joe and I looked at each other and burst out laughing. Like I said, you had to be there.

52

Diving through a Huey

Some things you have to see to believe, and some things you have to do to believe. Well, I did something myself, so of course, I saw it and I knew I did it, but to this day, it's hard to believe.

Let me back up a couple of years prior to this event. I was playing college basketball, and one of the reasons I got to play a good bit was because I could jump.

Back to my unbelievable event. A certain Captain who was a Huey pilot (some of you will guess who this genius was) had seen a pack on a trail. The Blues had been on the ground and were approaching the Huey on it's right and we piled on. This pilot was in the left front seat, and looking out, he saw this pack laying in a trail that moved away and to his left.

I had already gotten my flight helmet on in anticipation of us getting out of there. Instead of flying away like any sane person would do, he hovered there and told me to hop off and retrieve the pack. This went against everything the Rangers taught us in NCO school. Don't pick up anything that is overly obvious. It's more than likely booby-trapped. An NVA pack laying in the middle of a trail—well, duh!

This fool insisted while I and my guys were hanging in the air like a piñata waiting to get smacked. I got off, and taking a direct order, I dashed up and grabbed the pack and ran back toward the chopper.

I don't know which pilot was flying the damn thing, but they had drifted up. By the time I was getting relatively close to the ship, I looked up and I was looking at the bottom of the skids. About that time, I heard the crack of an AK-47. The gunner on that side opened up with his M-60 machine gun. Adrenaline, coupled with fear, made me take a couple more long strides then jump.

The skids were well above my head and the deck of the Huey is substantially higher than the skids. My swag (*scientific wild ass guess*) is that the deck was about ten feet off the ground. Remember, I was wearing all my regular gear including water, ammo, grenades, and a heavy radio. I got my M-16 in one hand and that stupid pack in the other.

Back to the jump. I took off and flew like Superman and landed on the deck on my stomach and, if one of the guys hadn't grabbed my web gear, I might have slid out the other side.

I did it and I saw myself do it, but it's still almost impossible to believe. I wasn't heroic—just plain scared.

There was nothing of consequence in the pack. I think the jerk just wanted a souvenir.

53

Cold at Landing Zone West

First, for those of you who don't know what a landing zone (LZ) was in Vietnam, here it is in a nutshell. The Army or Marines would pick out an area where they wanted to place a small base. They would clear it off, then they would put a defensive perimeter around it.

The Americal Division, of which I was a part, had many LZs, and because of the terrain, most were on the very top of a mountain. This meant they were high up and sometimes very high. The business we took care of was usually down in the valleys or on the lower slopes. Vietnam is well down in the tropics, so by location, it can be hot. Sometimes it was hot as hell. One hundred degrees was pretty common, and over one hundred ten degrees happened more than we wanted.

A mission had us on the ground in a valley that was full of water-filled, muddy rice paddies. Walking through knee-deep mud on an extraordinarily hot day will make you sweat like a race horse. We were soaking wet, then we got shot at. Adrenaline pushed the sweat factor over the top.

The enemy broke off and we searched the area we had been put in to check out. The Hueys came in and extracted us, and we headed back to our forward base at Tam Ky. Flying back after a mission was a good feeling, and we were pleased to be heading in.

Before we had gone too far, we got a radio message saying that a long-range reconnaissance patrol (LRRP) was in trouble, and they had to be extracted *now* or they might not survive. We were the closest helicopters and our pilots were diverted to this extraction.

Of course they had to get us off the Huey so the LRRPs could get on. So they flew up through a cloud layer and then to the top of LZ West. We jumped off, and the pilots and the gunners left on their new mission. They said they would come get us when they could.

Well, the valley we had just been in was one hundred seventeen degrees according to one of the pilots. As noted before, we were soaking wet. Within a matter of minutes, we were dumped into temperatures at least forty or fifty degrees cooler than the valley we just left, and we were wet right down to our socks.

In my lifetime, of course, I have encountered colder real temperatures, but never have I felt colder. We started to shiver almost immediately, and it wasn't long before my teeth started to chatter so hard I truly felt they would crack. The guys permanently stationed at LZ West looked at us like we were nuts. I would have told them to go to hell if I could have talked, but that wasn't possible. But, as it is often stated in the Army, you find sympathy in the dictionary right between shit and syphilis.

The choppers finally returned to pick us up. They also looked at us like we were nuts. It was literally hard to get up, and nobody was looking forward to a twenty- to thirty-minute ride in a helicopter with the wind blowing through. One of the coldest days in my life—in the tropics no less.

54

Friendly Fire

Not everything goes as planned. That is an understatement, especially when you are talking about combat operations.

Upon my return from R&R in Hawaii, I got the word from the jeep driver who picked me up at the airport that the Blues had taken a hard hit. When I got to the troop area, the details were just plain awful. Anella and Perry were dead, and Linker was severely injured.

In a nutshell, a Cobra pilot made a terrible decision. He fired rockets without being clear about where the Blues were located on the ground. He killed my guys and I was mad, sad, and disappointed. The Cobra pilots I had worked with were good and dependable. They were daring, but not careless. The pilot in command when this happened was one of those people who could be described as "seldom right, but never in doubt."

You can screw up in a business and lose money. You can mess up in sports and lose a game, but in combat, lives are the cost of stupidity. The loss of people KIA by the enemy is hurtful, but this screwup was maddening to me.

As I stated more than once in these writings, these are my observations from my viewpoint as a squad leader in the Blues. You can probably tell that I am still distressed after all these years. The pain of losing someone as good as Jim Anella was terrible at the time, and it really doesn't abate much after the passage of a significant number of years. Friendly fire incidents have happened in every war, and they will continue for as long as there is conflict.

I wish there was a significant thought to close this piece with, but there just isn't. "Friendly fire"—what a strange name for something that causes such havoc.

55

It Just Came Apart

We had done four combat assaults in one day. Luckily, we took no fire going in on any of them. But you, as a BlueGhost, don't know if an assault is going to be hot or not. Your blood pumps, and as we said, your butt puckers up. You've got no way to guess what the outcome is going to be as you are gliding into these potential hellholes. We would rate missions on the pucker factor from one to ten.

Headed back to base, our outstanding commanding officer saw something he felt should be checked out. That meant insert the Blues. We turned and headed to the spot. Just as we started our glide downwind, the whole area we were going to just came apart. Trees were flying into the air, dirt clods being thrown all over, and smoke and dust were thick.

Our pilots peeled off, and as they did, we looked on the horizon and here comes a battalion of troops carried by a huge number of Hueys. A coordinated bombardment from several different fire bases had hit the area where we were just headed. This was pre-planned to soften the area for the battalion assault.

If we had gotten there one minute earlier, no one would have survived. Two Hueys, their crews, and all the Blues would have been gone. Our CO at that time didn't check with brigade or division. Someone should have hung for that, but officers can be like lawyers sometimes. They don't eat their own.

56

Snatch Missions

Snatch Mission—isn't that a unique name for a military activity? The name describes exactly what we would do on these adventures. The people at division intelligence would decide that they needed to know more about what was going on in a certain geographic location. They came up with the idea to literally "snatch" someone from that area, bring them in, and interrogate them.

The implementation of this idea fell to F Troop Eighth Cavalry BlueGhost. The unit accomplished this mission in various ways. I will tell you how it was done when the Blues were involved.

Three or four of the Blues would mount a Huey and head to the predetermined area and look for someone to snatch. Sometimes there would be a Loach scouting around, and sometimes Cobras would be close by. Other times it was only us.

Someone would be spotted, usually a farmer plowing behind a water buffalo, and we would swoop down. We got off and ran to the guy and we would grab him and haul him back to the helicopter and off we'd go. He had been snatched.

We normally flew back to division headquarters at Chu Lai and turned the person over to the intel group. That was all we did in this scheme.

I know that spy craft and other forms of intelligence gathering have made a big difference in previous wars, and I know that it was deemed necessary. As an infantryman, my point of view was it felt like kidnapping. Put yourself in the farmer's place.

The rest I learned about snatch missions came from trickle-down hearsay. We were told the snatchees were returned to the place from which they were taken, given a little money, and told to have a nice life.

How they were treated was also the stuff of speculation and conjecture. The Americans would interrogate them, and sometimes we heard they were handed over to the South Vietnamese Army to be questioned further. The treatment they got from the ARVN was rumored to be stout, bordering on torture. To make matters worse for the unlucky participants in the process was that when they were returned home, the North Vietnamese Army (NVA) or the Vietcong would want to know what had been divulged to their enemies. Kid gloves were probably not used in this inquiry.

Snatch missions—just another day at the office.

57

The Mongoose Event

My good friend Roger Caruthers was a country boy and used some of those skills in Vietnam in a very unique way.

At our rear base at Chu Lai, we stayed in rectangular buildings we called hooches. These hooches were fairly close to the beach on the South China Sea. There was a small strip of thick jungle between the hooches and the beach, and this strip of vegetation contained some interesting wildlife.

One day, someone spotted a monkey, and Roger got word of the sighting. He took it as a challenge to capture the monkey, and he came up with a true country boy remedy for this problem. Roger and I both came from parts of the world where building and setting out rabbit boxes was a way of life and was done to catch rabbits to eat.

A rabbit box is essentially a long wooden tube with a drop-down door attached to the back interior of the tube with a string. Food is put in the back of the box so that when a rabbit went to the back of the box, a trip was released, dropping the door, thereby catching the rabbit.

Well, Roger had to be field expedient, as we said in the army, and he came up with a box that worked on the same principle. He took a foot locker, sawed the lid in half, nailed down half the top, and left the other half free to open and close. Roger got some fruit from the mess hall and put it in the covered half of the foot locker. He rigged the fruit so that when the monkey got in to grab the fruit, the other half of the foot locker top would drop. Roger had put a nail through the edge of the top so that it would "nail" itself closed when it fell.

Well, Roger got his device into position down in the strip of jungle. It sat there for a while. I don't remember how long, but one night, the wham of the slamming top was heard, and Roger knew he had the monkey. The foot locker was tied by a rope and hauled up the hill out into the middle of the road that went through our troop area.

A mosquito net was acquired and draped over the foot locker and several of our platoon members were drafted (again) to stand on the edges of the net to keep the monkey from getting away. Roger used a long rod to slip through the net and pry the top open. This all worked fine, and out came the monkey. The only problem was, it wasn't a monkey—it was a mongoose.

This thing came out of the foot locker like a brown streak and circled the box about three times before all the war heroes could take off running. Roger kept his wit about him enough to give a wild kick at the mongoose that knocked it out. He was able to pick it up by its tail. I took pictures as I had been designated as the photographer. This becomes important years later.

The story of this adventure made the rounds in the troop for a short time and then faded into history, or so I thought.

Roger got shot a few months later and was sent to Japan, then stateside to spend years in various hospitals. He finally made it back to East Tennessee and spent the bulk of his adult life in a wheelchair. He has done amazing things with his life, but that's a story for another time.

I finished my tour and went home to Georgia. Having attempted to find Roger a couple of times with no luck, I was about to give up. Later, in the late eighties and early nineties, I moved to Chattanooga. This was around the time the internet started getting strong, and it helped me find Roger and several other troop members.

Earlier, I said my taking pictures of the mongoose event would be important. Let me explain. When Roger and I actually got together, we were delighted to renew our friendship and talk of old times. The thing that thrilled Roger the most was when he learned I still had pictures of the "Great Mongoose Capture" and the "Great Mongoose Escape."

The reason this meant so much to Roger was because he had told his story to many of his VFW buddies, and he said he had the definite feeling they didn't believe him. Roger would not rest until he took my pictures to the VFW and verified this great story to that crowd.

The monkey/mongoose story had come full cycle.

THE GREAT MONGOOSE CAPTURE
Prior to THE GREAT MONGOOSE ESCAPE.

Joe Delong and Roger Caruthers holding the Mongoose by the tail.

58

Tracers in the Air

The term *tracer* means a bullet that has been coated with a material that makes the bullet glow when shot out of a gun barrel. The use for a tracer is so that the shooter can tell where the bullets are going and adjust fire to be more accurately on target. When loading ammo in clips, we usually put every fourth round as a tracer. Machine gunners did the same thing when putting ammo belts together.

The object behind this piece is to try to describe how it is to be shot at by tracer fire high up in the air. As we had completed a mission and were headed back to Chu Lai, we were flying pretty high, out of reach of most small arms. All of a sudden, as I just happened to be looking at a spot on the ground, a red glow showed up and tracers started coming up at us. It was a fifty-caliber machine gun that was capable of ruining our day.

I'd been shot at on the ground many times and it is not a good thing, but I had my M-16 and I felt I could respond. I had some control over that situation. Being shot at in a Huey as a passenger is totally different. The feeling to me was one of dumbfounded fear. Either they got you or they missed. There was no way to respond to that guy down there. The tracers came up and went by. They looked like red footballs going by. He would squeeze off another burst that would zip by. It was hard to tell how close they really were. This went on for probably a few seconds but felt like an eternity to me.

We flew on until we were out of range, and I felt as wrung out as I did after any firefight I was ever in.

The next time you see action footage of American or British bombers during World War II, I want you to think of those crews. Sometimes they would be under attack by German fighter aircraft or ground base anti-aircraft fire for hours. After my short-lived experience of being the fish in the barrel, my admiration for those men is boundless.

The scenery could be beautiful as a Huey flies in the mountains.

59

We All Missed the Guy

The seven steady hold factors is a set of principles the Army uses in trying to teach how to shoot a rifle. You hear it in Basic, AIT, and NCO school. If there was any inkling in my mind of those factors now, I would tell you, but I can't.

The Blues were on the ground, and we were moving across an area that was pretty open. I and three others were side by side spaced out with about five yards between us. I heard the distinctive sound of bullets zipping by and then two definite cracks of an AK-47. They make an undeniable sound like the pop of a super-large cap pistol.

The offending VC jumped up about thirty yards in front of us and took off running over flat ground with no cover close by. We all put our M-16s to our shoulders and started shooting. We missed. Some genius among us said, "Well, I guess we didn't use the seven steady hold factors."

That VC was one lucky puppy. We often talked about that little adventure. We still could not believe we missed the guy.

60

Willie Williams

Willie changed my life. It's as simple as that. Willie came to the BlueGhost several months after my arrival and came as an infantryman replacement.

Right here, let me back up and tell you a little about my history. I was born in Atlanta and grew up all my young years through high school at Fairburn, Georgia, about twenty miles south of Atlanta. This was in the late forties, all of the fifties, and part of the sixties. This was the Deep South in more ways than one.

The south I grew up in was strictly segregated in every way. Separate schools, separate rest rooms, separate water fountains. This was okay with me because, as a kid, I didn't know any different. It didn't even register with me that the kids of a black family that lived behind us had to leave an hour and a half earlier than me and get home an hour and a half later because they had to go almost to Atlanta to get to school. Separate but equal. I kinda doubt it.

Practically everybody in my little universe used the "N" word. I used the "N" word. It was common, and if you can believe it, it was seldom used with malice. That's just the way things were. Someone would say there goes a "N" man, or who is that "N" woman. A very unfortunate adjective.

You had to have experienced that era, and it is still perplexing to try and explain my actions and thoughts back then. My intent was not hurtful or malicious when I said some of that stuff, but I can sure see how it would be taken that way.

Enough of my soapbox. The Army doesn't care if you are orange, purple, white, or black. It sees you as green. The Army was my first exposure to total integration and it was an eye opener. That time in our country was rife with racial tension and confrontation. But, like I said, the Army thinks green.

Getting back to Willie. Shortly after his placement in the Blues, it was obvious everybody liked Willie and he had leadership quality out the yin-yang. He would talk to anyone and that's how I came to discover what a special man he was. He would talk about some of the things I've noted earlier in this piece, and he would talk about how hurtful and degrading some of that stuff could be.

The thing was we never got angry. I don't even know if we solved anything. It was just two southern boys kicking the can around. I don't know how much it helped him, but there's no doubt it helped me.

A few years ago, right before Willie died from diabetes, I was able to reach him by phone and tell him what an effect he had on me. Orange, purple, white, or black, Willie was a good man.

Willie Williams and John Sanders.

61

Rockets into Chu Lai

After a while, I had been out on several combat assaults and seen some action regarding the enemy. It was exhilarating and frightening with many other emotions mixed in, but during direct combat as an infantryman, I felt I had some degree of control and I could fight back. After all, I was carrying an M-16 and a radio whereby I could request Cobra gunships to bring hell on the enemy.

We were rocketed one day at the main base at Chu Lai. The rockets they fired were about the equivalent of a 155 artillery shell. That is to say they were fairly large and powerful.

Let me say this with no fear of contradiction, rocket fire will scare the hell out of you. If you're lucky, you hear it screaming over your head and land somewhere behind you. If you don't hear them until they explode, they are close by or out in front. The thing that frightens you so bad is that they are totally indiscriminate and random. Once it starts, there is not a thing you can do except try to find some coverage. You will run, crawl, scramble, and wish you could fly to find some form of relative safety, be it a sandbagged bunker or a ditch.

When it's over, you try to regain composure and assure yourself that you were cool. That is just after you looked down to make sure you didn't wet yourself.

62

Smoke Grenade by LZ West

The Blues, the infantry platoon, were used in a variety of missions. We once were asked to provide security for people that were trying to monitor enemy movement. The way they planned to do this was by burying boxes that had a detector sticking out of the top that looked like a blade of grass. When someone walked by on a trail, the detector would note the movement. The box would send a message to a monitor and the count was tallied.

We would fly out with these guys, be inserted, and then walk to a spot that had been predesignated to plant one of these devices. We would then set up a perimeter around these people while they worked. Sounds pretty straightforward, doesn't it?

We had just gotten a new guy assigned to the Blues and he was with us on this mission. New guys tended to be a little nervous on their first time out, but this guy was also stupid. He had attached his grenades to his web gear *by the ring pulls!* He had compounded things by not bending back the ends of the pull pins. The sheer weight of the grenades in conjunction with his movements made one of the grenades slide down its pin until it fell to the ground.

When a grenade and its pin separate, a handle flies off, and the countdown begins until the grenade goes off. Well, we heard the distinctive sound of a grenade losing its handle and the *thunk* sound of a grenade hitting the ground. Several people yelled, "Hit the dirt!" and we all did.

We lay there waiting for the explosion of a grenade that we all knew was close by because we had heard it hit the ground. Time went by, and we heard the hiss of a smoke grenade spewing out grape-colored smoke. He had just marked our position for anybody with eyes within five miles to spot us. Thank God, it wasn't a frag grenade.

Well, the Sergeants gently inquired what the f__k just happened? A quick investigation uncovered the guilty party and his errors corrected. Two of the frags had slipped halfway down their pins.

By the next day the sensors that had been installed had all quit working. They sent us back out with the guys who had activated them to see what happened. Two were completely gone and three were booby-trapped and had to be blown in place.

Technology and stupidity seldom work well together.

63

Time Goes Away

Some of the things I've written about here were of a short time and I am sure of that. But when it comes to some of the more involved and intense actions, there is no way I can even hazard a guess as to their duration.

Once, a few years ago, I was reading a book about the battle at Antietam in Maryland during the Civil War. Two union soldiers were side by side on the edge of a place called the cornfield. It changed hands many times during the battle, and it has been written that at battle's end, you could walk over the field without touching the ground. When each fight started and all those rifles fired the smoke and dust were so thick, you could hardly see.

One of those soldiers asked his buddy, "What time is it?"

The other said, "It's nine o'clock."

And the first man asked, "In the morning or at night?"

That's how far away the concept of time can get from you.

64

Sound of a Huey

For those of you that were there, I don't have to tell you how distinctive the sound of a Huey was. To this day, I can't find the words to describe it so that a novice would understand. All I can say as a member of the Blues, it was a very, very welcome sound when the Hueys were coming to pick us up after a mission.

Opportunities to see or hear a Huey were rare after the war until Greg Whitehurst of the Blues from Griffin, Georgia, told me about an organization at Hampton, Georgia. The group is the "Army Aviation Heritage Association" (www.armyav.org). They are dedicated to maintaining and flying Vietnam-era aircraft. Their hangars are at Tara Field right behind Atlanta International Speedway. These folks fly at airshows and other events, and for a fee, you can fly with them. They fly Hueys and Cobras. Go to their website and see the calendar as to when and where.

The hangars are available most days, and they welcome walk-ins. During the BlueGhost reunion in Peachtree City, Georgia, a huge group went over to visit them. It was great.

I've taken my wife, my grandson, godsons, and several others to fly on a Huey, and it has been a thrill for all of them. My grandson says it's the most fun he ever had. One of my godsons says he wants to be a pilot. My wife probably had the most unique take on her flight.

She said, "John, you have been lying to me about Vietnam. All you did was fly around and have fun."

Dave Harrigan, Norm Gravino and a rainbow.
Quite a picture.

65

Rotating Home

This is a unique time in any Vietnam veterans' life. You have made it through a year and you win the prize—you're going back to "the world." This sounds pretty straightforward and it can be, but let me take you through the last part of my tour of duty in the Americal Division.

First of all, we had a practice in the Blues platoon that if someone made to the point where they only had thirty days left in country, we did not make them go out on missions with the exception of dire circumstances. Two reasons for this: It would just be plain horrible to have someone killed or wounded in their last few days, and secondly, is that people, including me, got so paranoid they were not good soldiers. You literally feel like there is a target on your back and a big red X on your forehead.

When you got close to going home, we called it "getting short." We kept short-timers' calendars, and each succeeding day was marked off in dramatic fashion. Some of the designs of these calendars was innovative. Another story for another time.

F Troop had a warrant officer pilot who had gotten down to his last few days. He had seen a huge amount of enemy contact from the pilot seat of a Loach (very low-flying helicopter). His perspective was that he had survived so many harrowing situations that he didn't want to cash in his chips at the very end. This drove him to hyper paranoia; he wore a flack vest and metal helmet everywhere he went. This all took place at division base camp, which was a pretty safe place. He would sit on the floor with his back to the heaviest duty wall he could find.

It may sound like I'm being critical of this man. I am not. He was just a real-life manifestation of what most of us felt. He made it home.

My last days in the F-Troop area were really unremarkable with the notable exception in that I got drunk. I mean stupid drunk. The blame for this goes mainly to Greg Yaramyshin because he caused me to be overserved. His bad influence brought me down.

I'm just kidding, Greg. He is really a great guy and we have remained fast friends through all these years. You had to be there. If ever there was a cause for celebration, that was the time. But, then again, my timing as to getting wasted was very poor to say the least. This all happened my last night as a BlueGhost. The next morning at 0600, I had to catch a flight at the airfield, which was a good distance from our HQ. A jeep was to shuttle me to the field and I had to meet it at 0500.

Get the picture: I was goofy drunk at midnight, sick all night, and in a jeep at 0500 going to catch a plane. When I say "catch a plane," I'm not talking about Delta Airlines. I am climbing into a C-130 with swinging net "seats"—if you can call them seats. Also, let me paint the picture of my takeoff from Chu Lai. It was summertime in Vietnam. The morning temperature was around ninety degrees, and the humidity felt like you are swimming. On top of this, backwash from the C-130 engines was blowing very hot air over me. Don't forget my self-induced condition at this time, then we had to climb up the back ramp and sit down in those suspended swinging seats. Most on the flight were also American soldiers, but there were South Vietnamese soldiers and a few civilians. Directly across from me was an old Vietnamese woman who had turned her gums fire-engine red and her teeth coal mine black by chewing beetle nut. Most all the old Vietnamese in the country chewed this stuff. To top it off, she was holding two small bamboo cages, each holding two small chickens. We took off and the old woman would smile, the chickens were constantly pooping, and I was sure I was going to die before ever reaching Cam Rahn Bay.

Luckily, there was a stop at Qui Nhan on the way south, and I am sure this stop saved my misguided life. No kidding. I had sat there seriously thinking of all the things I had survived that year and here my hungover dumb ass was going to die on this plane. When they let the ramp down on that C-130 and that fresh air rushed in, it was like when you break the surface of the water as the air in your lungs was about to run out. We got out and walked around a bit then we boarded, and thank goodness, chicken lady did not come back on board. The rest of the flight was uneventful.—I was going to live.

At Cam Rahn Bay, which was one of the main entrance and exit points for Americans during the war, I spent almost two full days sitting in a barracks with nothing to do, nothing to read, and nothing to fill my time. The Army, in its wisdom, could have flown me on to Ft. Lewis and the world, but no, it was one more hot day in the exotic Far East for me.

I finally got on a big jet (not pink) headed home. The stories you hear about the big yell all the guys made when the plane's wheels left the ground in Vietnam is true. It was remarkable.

At Ft. Lewis, they really did feed us a very good steak dinner on arrival. Within a day, I processed out of the Army, got issued a dress green uniform (two sizes too small), and was ferried to the Seattle Airport headed to Atlanta. I was a civilian again.

Reunions

As I write this, it is 2017, forty-seven years after leaving Vietnam. The last birthday I celebrated made me seventy—damn, that's just not right.

Overall, my luck has been pretty good, and one of the real bright spots has been reunions. After the unofficial reunion in Atlanta, we have had seventeen reunions of the F Troop Eighth Cavalry Vietnam Veterans Association. We meet all around the United States, and it's great seeing fellow BlueGhosts. Also, it is so rewarding to see other parts of this spectacular country.

Friendships, camaraderie, and a genuine caring for each other have been hallmarks of these get-togethers, not only for us ex-soldiers but for the spouses and various family members that have attended. Maybe one of the most important attributes is in one word—healing. Speaking for me, there is no doubt that mental healing has happened at these functions. It follows that physical improvements come after mental health progress.

I love our reunions. They feed my soul.

The following is a welcoming statement I made at a BlueGhost reunion during my three-year stint as president of the BlueGhost Veterans Association:

How many are newbies?

Good to see familiar faces.

Why do we come to reunions?

Many played sports, band, chorus, clubs, student government, or other groups. Later, you may have been in civic groups, clubs, or like Carl, a gang.

Nothing compares to F/8th BlueGhost. When you're part of an organization that is playing for the highest stakes, you bond. Whether you realize it at the time or not. Some of us were literally flying out to kill or be killed. Some were turning wrenches, reading meters, checking wiring, or setting torque. *All* the jobs in BlueGhost were important because if any of us did not do his assignment right, it would result in American blood on the ground. Make that BlueGhost blood.

I knew some of you in Vietnam, but the bulk of you I have gotten to know at these reunions. We were there as a unit from the mid-sixties to the early seventies. We were steeped in the same teapot, no matter when we were there.

Sometime back, there was a burial service at Arlington for three BlueGhost lost in '72 in the shoot down of a scout helicopter. The site was found and remains were identified. Through the efforts of Jack Kennedy, Gus Gustavson, and others, there was a large turnout of BlueGhost from all eras. I wish all of you could have seen what it meant to family members to have us there. It was also important among the BlueGhost who attended to support each other.

Many of you knew Roger Caruthers from the blues in '69. He was shot and damaged severely and spent his post-war life in a wheelchair. These reunions meant the world to Roger, and he came until health prevented his attendance. All who knew him admired and looked forward to seeing him at these meetings.

Roger died this past Thanksgiving and eleven BlueGhosts came to his service in Rockwood, Tennessee. The community and his family were blown away at this showing. They also had a good time hearing "Roger" stories from Vietnam and the reunions.

There are so many good things that have come from this association, including the things I just mentioned and the healing that has happened among us.

We care for each other in a way that is hard to explain. We also have a bond with the widows and near widows of our comrades, along with family members who we've met at these get-togethers.

I'm so glad all of you are here. Get to know everyone you can and have a good time.

See you in Chattanooga!

The first unofficial reunion in Atlanta.
Left to right: Bob Wiggins, Joe Loadholtes, John (Doc)Anderson,
Roger Caruthers, Charles Francis, Greg Yaramishyn, John W. Harris,
William (Pappy) Patterson.
(photo by Ben Arp)

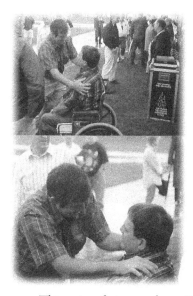
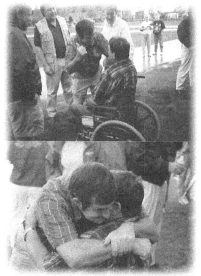

This series of pictures shows Ken Wilson seeing Roger Caruthers
for the first time since November of '69. Ken helped put Roger
on Phil King's Huey for evacuation after Roger was shot.
(photos by Ben Arp)

67

A Letter to the Troops

Following is a letter I wrote at the early stages of the U.S. efforts to rid the world of Saddam Hussein. He had invaded Kuwait and was threatening Saudi Arabia. Our troops had been sent to Saudi Arabia for a buildup prior to taking action against Iraq.

There was much in the news about the anticipation the American soldiers were feeling. The continued training and the boredom of waiting to go into action was tough on the troops. Requests were broadcast for the public to write letters to the troops or send encouraging cards and notes. These were sent to no specific person. There was an address given where to send the letters with the assurance they would be distributed randomly to service members in the Middle East.

My experience in BlueGhost made me feel I might be able to contribute something that could be helpful and instructive. With the letter written, I made ten copies and sent them on their way.

The response was gratifying and surprising. There were six replies of varying lengths and one was most interesting. A Marine sergeant said he was so taken with the letter that he showed it to his commanding officer. His CO posted the letter by his headquarters and instructed everyone to read it.

All I can hope is that some of the BlueGhost training and experience from 1969 and 1970 may have helped some folks of a different generation survive their war. Here is that letter:

Dear Friend,

First of all, let me say thank you and I appreciate what you are doing. Hussein is a true nutcase, and he must be checked now or you will have to go back later and it will be worse. Also, the U.S. has got to take a stand so the rest of the world won't think we are paper tigers and cannot be depended on.

All that is easy for me to say when it's your butt on the line, but let me tell you that I have been there. I arrived in Vietnam on my twenty-second birthday as a drafted infantryman. Having gone through NCO school, I arrived as an E-5 squad leader assigned to an air cavalry "Blue Team." Later, I was platoon sergeant and, at twenty- two, was the "old guy" other than my platoon leader; he was twenty-three.

Our mission was to get out downed aircraft and pilots and to go on search-and-destroy missions. I'm not writing this to tell you a bunch of war stories. This is to give you advice from someone who knows what going to war is really about. As I stated before, I was drafted, so I was not the most military guy you will meet, but I did learn that you *must* pay attention to detail. Lots of people got killed because they didn't keep their equipment up, didn't know where they were on a map, or didn't use basic common sense. War is very unforgiving of people who are just plain stupid.

The boredom has got to be rough, but keep your gear ready as if you were going to fight in the next minute. There is nothing worse than equipment failure when your *life* is on the line.

Next, don't be afraid to admit to yourself that you are scared. All the *Rambo* movies are a bunch of crap. Real war is a scary thing, and your enemy will not be a bunch of incompetent boobs. I was proud of the way I functioned most of the time, but there were some situations when I got so scared, I had to make myself breathe.

As you know, we didn't have public support to the extent that you do now. We had to generate our own support among ourselves. I did learn something you should know and that is when one of us got hurt or killed, the rest of us got truly fired up, and at that time, American soldiers are the most aggressive and best fighters in the world. You have the country's support and you have an enemy who truly needs his butt kicked. Take advantage of this.

Of all the armies I have observed or studied about, if I had to choose the people I would least want to fight, it is the Americans. When motivated, we can be very good at getting the enemies attention. Be good at what you do. Don't forget once fighting starts, the object is to kill people and break things. Make it so bad for them that they will give up the fight. I want *you* to come home alive and well.

If there is something I can do for you, let me know.

Sincerely,
John W. Harris

68

Roger's Story After the War

I've made mention of Roger Caruthers several times in this narrative. He got to BlueGhost several months prior to my arrival, but he took the same route—drafted, basic, AIT, NCO school, and then Vietnam. He was on a mission as a squad leader in November 1969 when he was shot. His wounds included spinal cord injury.

Let me say a little about that incident at this time because it had influence on Roger's life years later. Two Hueys flew the Blues to the site that day, and one was piloted by Phil King. Very soon after Roger got on the ground, he was shot. Phil just made a short loop, and he and his crew flew back into, what was by then, a very hot situation. They got Roger loaded and literally flew like a bat out of hell to get Roger to the field surgeons at Hawk Hill. It saved Roger's life.

He made it to the evacuation hospital at Chu Lai, then to Japan, and eventually to Walter Reed Hospital in the States. Roger spent years in and out of VA hospitals and endured too many surgeries to count. As for myself, I was going about my post-war life. There were two more years of college, a degree in engineering, an expanding family, and getting on with life. I had lost track of Roger.

Several years later, I decided to try and find some of the men from BlueGhost. Roger was first on my list.

The inception of the internet made searching for, and finding people, a whole lot easier. It was a thrill to find Roger and realize he was only an hour and a half up the road from me. He was at Rockwood, Tennessee, and I am at Chattanooga.

The day I had set up to go see Roger I told my wife, Eve, that I would be back early that afternoon. I got back after midnight. Roger and I talked and talked and talked. It was the first time I saw the power of reunion.

Roger was always so positive about things, and he loved a good joke and good stories better than anybody. Despite constant pain in his legs and being mostly wheelchair-bound, he did remarkable things. There was an old family farm that was quite large. He had a fellow, Benny, that did most of the physical work, but Roger managed everything. They raised cattle, beans, pumpkins, etc.

Remarkably, Roger had rigged a hydraulic arm in the back of his truck that would aid him to get from his truck to a four-wheeler. He drove like it was NASCAR all over the farm, and he would herd cattle. He called them his "girls."

Those of you reading this who knew Roger would easily detect his upper East Tennessee style of talking. Trust me, Roger was no hick. I've told several people that Roger was smarter than all of us put together, and I don't know specifics about his finances, but suffice to say, he did well.

But what Roger did best was people. He was on his area's Boy Scout Council. He went to elementary schools teaching flag etiquette. Later, he was very active in his VFW post.

In my eyes, his crowning glory was about his nieces. Their names are Georgia, Marny, and Jennifer and they are the daughters of Roger's brother. The brother had several circumstances, too complicated to explain here, that kept him out of the girls' lives for the most part.

Although the girl's mother, Sheila, is a wonderful person and a great lady, the girls needed help when it came to going to college. Roger's financial and motivational help prompted all three of these ladies to get bachelor's and advanced degrees.

They are brilliant people and are doing super things. One is on a mission for the United Nations in Africa, another is teaching higher mathematics at a university, and the third is a CPA. Roger has got to be smiling down on this.

A story to tell you a little about Roger's outlook and perspective follows. He often suffered from bedsores as you can imagine with his physical situation being what it was. One time it got bad enough to require surgery. Eve and I went to Memphis during this episode to visit him at the VA hospital. He was in post op laying on top of an open mesh webbing with sand under it and warm air blowing through the sand.

We walked in the room to see Roger with a computer in his lap. He saw us and quickly put up a hand to stop us and then held up one finger, indicating he wanted us to give him a minute. Afterward, he said he was sorry but he was "timing the market." If you are not familiar with timing the stock market, it is a technique used by very smart people and it's not for sissies. A lot of money is made and lost this way. I never had the nerve or the money to try it.

Roger was one of the earliest and most enthusiastic reunion participants among BlueGhost. He was at the first unofficial reunion in Atlanta. His enthusiasm and mere presence inspired everyone there, and from then on, he was a major participant until he could no longer physically go. The BlueGhost organization owes him a great deal.

Roger got a lot back from the group in return. He renewed old relationships with those that were with him in 1969, but he loved getting to know BlueGhost from all eras of F/8.

One especially important tie that was renewed was between Roger and Phil King. Earlier I told you about Phil's return into fire to get Roger out. Move forward about thirty years when BlueGhost reunions started and soon after that Phil got involved. It wasn't long until Roger and Phil created a friendship to be admired. Next were visits by Phil and his wonderful wife Jean (Phil *way* over married) to Roger's home in Rockwood and farm at Clarkrange.

To show you the style and character that was Roger Caruthers, he couldn't go to Indiana but he sent a whole HoneyBaked Ham to Phil and Jean during the holidays. A note said he wanted Phil's family to eat this ham and know that they were dining with a hero. Can you imagine?

He was such a wonderful friend to me and Eve. As many of you read this, I know you are recollecting stories about Roger or stories told by Roger. He was probably the best storyteller in all of BlueGhost.

For those who did not get to know him, it's your loss, but whenever you encounter something good or inspiring, try to think of Roger and give a little nod or a wink upward. He would like that.

Me and Sgt. Caruthers. November, 1969
A few days before Roger was shot.

69

Notice about Roger's Death

This is a note that I posted online notifying the group about Roger Caruther's death:

> I am sad to report that our comrade, and my dear friend, Roger Caruthers passed away on Thanksgiving Day at 11:15pm.
>
> For those of you who knew Roger from previous reunions, he was certainly a treat to be around. We all loved to hear him tell stories. Nobody could tell a story like Roger.
>
> For those who did not have the opportunity to know him, you missed a chance to be uplifted by just being around him. He was a fixture at our earlier reunions, and he looked forward to all the reunions he was able to attend. He stated that he anticipated the reunions more than anything. Sadly, his physical decline made him miss the last few.
>
> My finding Roger several years ago was one of the seeds that caused us to get together in Atlanta for that first unofficial reunion. The efforts of Joe and Mary Loadholtes, Doc and Linda Anderson, Bob Wiggins, and others

pushed onward from there and the BlueGhost Association grew.

I feel confident in saying that all involved in those early days were inspired by Roger. For those of you who did not get to meet Roger, he was severely wounded during a mission with the Blues in late 1969. His injuries were serious, with spinal cord involvement, and he spent many years in and out of the hospital. His mobility was mostly via wheelchair.

Roger never complained. I would go and see him thinking to help him feel better, and I would be the one inspired by him. His example made me ashamed to complain about a headache. I will bet the farm that all of you who knew him are saying the same thing.

Roger never married, but had a great family. He essentially raised his three nieces and put them all through college and advanced degrees.

Physically, Roger was diminished, but we should all strive to be half the man he was. If we do, we could report job well done.

Roger requested to be cremated and his ashes spread on his beloved family farm. I will keep you posted on this site about when the service will be. The early speculation was about two weeks.

Rest in Peace, Dear Friend.

70

Why Did You Go and Leave Me?

I was driving down the road when gravity came through the road, through the floorboard, and into my feet. It made me stop and write this down.

Why did ya'll go and leave me?
I'm still here; mostly lived a good life
And it's been a long time without you.
The wonder is always there.
What would you be doing with your life
Back here in "the world" we all longed for?
I still ache sometimes at the wonder of that.
Would you be the pilot in the jet overhead?
Would you be my buddy down the street?
Maybe a politician? Some of you were good at BS.
Your families surely miss you.
I've met some of them.
You're talked about at reunions.
Your names are said out loud.
We still remember.
But still the question is there.
Why did you go and leave me?
You were all good people and they say there is a grand plan.
When somebody figures that out, let me know.

If there is anything good about "only the good
die young"
Again, I need to know.

Afterword

People didn't know how to take me when I returned home. My family and wife's extended family were glad to see me. There were many hugs and happy handshakes, but after that, it was like being handled with kid gloves.

I felt everyone was wondering if I was going to get back to "normal," or was there going to be something crazy or violent? The news media was already depicting Vietnam veterans in a negative light, and it only got worse as time moved on. The antiwar crowd was already in high gear and that was hard to deal with. To hear me and my comrades talked about in such hurtful and derogatory ways was downright painful. Several of my fellow soldiers had given their lives in the last few months, and other good friends were still over there.

It's not my style to go to the streets and confront the protesters, so I withdrew. Prior to getting drafted, I had been in junior college for two years, and while I was gone, they had expanded and were offering a bachelor's degree. They accepted me so I went back to college. If you are going to withdraw, an engineering college is not a bad place to go. Those people are serious.

This turned out to be one of my best post-war moves. The campus was half veterans. Many guys were just like me. They had been there before and then gotten drafted, and now they wanted that four-year degree with help from the GI Bill. This series of events was a true blessing for me and these other student vets. We formed a veterans club and we had regular meetings and social events.

The informal talking with these Vietnam veterans was so therapeutic at the time, and I don't think anyone realized it until much later. PTSD wasn't even on the radar at that time. This period of my life gave me time to decompress and do it with likeminded veterans who didn't have to handle me with kid gloves. Looking back, my heart goes out to guys who came back home and went right into life with no mechanism to decompress.

When I say there was withdrawal, that doesn't mean I went underground. My immediate family and basketball kept me involved in life. That may sound a little goofy that basketball helped me stay in one piece.

Let me explain. When I got back, I still had two years of college athletic eligibility left. My coach, Harry Lockhart, renewed my scholarship plus I had the GI Bill, so I was literally making money and going to school. The rough part was after the first two practices, it became painfully apparent my back would not let me function at a level needed to play competitive college basketball.

I said several times in these pieces that I am a lucky fellow. Well, here again my luck held up. Coach Lockhart called me to his office and instead of taking my scholarship or reducing it he asked me to help coach defense and scout opponent's games. He never mentioned changing my scholarship in any way.

Harry Lockhart had a rough, gruff exterior, but his heart was as big as all outdoors and he came through for me when it really counted. Harry was a great man. Many years later, the phrase "pay it forward" came into the vernacular, and I realized that he had beat them to the draw. God bless Coach Harry Lockhart.

Life moved on in its many facets. My second daughter was born, and my professional life progressed to eventually let me retire (almost).

Around the turn of the century, our BlueGhost Veterans Association was started and annual reunions followed. These reunions are another part of my luck along with luck for practically every BlueGhost involved. Without hesitation, I will say that many, many lives have been changed for the better by these reunions and some lives may have been saved. This also includes spouses, children, siblings, and friends.

A few times in these writings, I said "you had to be there." Well, I guess that sums up the F Troop Eighth Cavalry BlueGhost experience. It is hoped these recordings of little snippets of our lives as

BlueGhost from the war to the present have captured the camaraderie, ingenuity, fear, humor, dread, terror, appreciation, grief, loneliness, and joy that has been a part of all of us as BlueGhost.

About the Author

John W. Harris grew up twenty miles south of Atlanta when that area was as rural as deep southern Georgia. His youth was spent going barefooted, riding bicycles, and playing cow pasture baseball. He was blessed to have a large number of caring aunts and uncles and a huge cadre of fun-loving cousins. His friends were a diversified lot who influenced him for good and bad.

His immediate family was a mother, father, and two sisters. His mother was the best ever. Some of you may think that your mom was the best, but you are confused. His was the best—period. Both his sisters passed away too soon, one at eight from cystic fibrosis and the other at sixty-four with ALS.

Outside of his family and BlueGhost comrades, his great love is basketball. He enjoys other sports, but he got to attend college because he could shoot a basketball. Many friends and wonderful experiences came to John because of this great game.

He received a letter in 1968 from his draft board that said, "Greetings." This started his Army and Vietnam story. Looking back on the segments of this story and with inquiries from his grandson, Frankie Reynolds, John was motivated to write this book.

John has lived on Lookout Mountain next to Chattanooga, Tennessee, for the last twenty-seven years with his wife, Eve, who has encouraged, cajoled, and prodded him to get these pieces on paper before they are lost to time.

CPSIA information can be obtained
at www.ICGtesting.com
Printed in the USA
LVHW09s0352201018
593971LV00002BA/2/P